Cinderella
meets the
Caveman

Dr. David E. Clarke

HARVEST HOUSE PUBLISHERS

EUGENE, OREGON

All Scripture references are taken from the New American Standard Bible®, © 1960, 1962, 1963, 1968, 1971, 1972, 1973, 1975, 1977, 1995 by The Lockman Foundation. Used by permission. (www.Lockman.org)

Dr. David E. Clarke: Published in association with the literary agent of Hartline Literary Agency, Pittsburgh, PA.

This book contains stories in which people's names and some details of their situations have been changed in order to protect their privacy.

Cover photo © altrendo images / Altrendo / Getty Images

Back cover author photo © Bob Baggett

Cover by Terry Dugan Design, Minneapolis, Minnesota

CINDERELLA MEETS THE CAVEMAN
Copyright © 2007 by Dr. David E. Clarke
Published by Harvest House Publishers
Eugene, Oregon 97402
www.harvesthousepublishers.com

Library of Congress Cataloging-in-Publication Data
Clark, David, Ph. D.
    Cinderella meets the caveman / David E. Clarke.
        p. cm.
    ISBN-13: 978-0-7369-1911-1
    ISBN-10: 0-7369-1911-2
    1. Marriage—Religious aspects—Christianity. 2. Man-woman relationships—Religious aspects—Christianity. 3. Boredom—Religious aspects—Christianity. I. Title
    BV835.C573 2007
    248.8'44—dc22

                                                    2006030435

Printed in the United States of America

07 08 09 10 11 12 13 14 15 / VP-SK / 11 10 9 8 7 6 5 4 3 2 1

To Sandy,

the most wonderful person in the world.

CONTENTS

PART THREE

How to Fight to Be Close

PART FOUR

How to Kill Your Rituals and Start Over

Part One

How You Built a
Boring Marriage

1

Our Passion Up and Left!

Boredom: The Number One Marriage Killer

The gibbon is a small primate found in southeastern Asia. It is one of the few mammals that mates for life. When two gibbons decide to tie the knot—*boom!*—it's permanent. These miniature monkeys take "until death do us part" seriously.

After a courtship that can last months, the male and female become a couple and move in together. They leave their families and settle down in an area of leafy trees, choosing one specific tree for their home tree.

You're thinking, *By mistake, have I picked up a* National Geographic *book on apes?* In a way, you have. But this is going to be about marriage. Trust me.

Few human beings are aware of the day-to-day life of the married gibbon couple. You will now join that privileged few. I can sense your excitement. Not only will you be able to amaze your friends with your knowledge, you'll learn something very significant about your own marriage.

Come with me now to the forests of southeastern Asia.

Just a Couple of Crazy Gibbons

Once they move into their home tree, the gibbons begin to practice a basic daily routine that they will follow without variation for the rest of their lives together.

Each morning just before dawn, the male and female gibbon rise and sing. Together, they belt out a song that can last up to two hours. They sing this same song the same way every morning.

The gibbon couple spends the rest of their day swinging from tree to tree in their area, looking for food. When they find food, they go through a cycle of eating, grooming, and resting. They groom each other the same way every time: The left hand parts the hair, and the right hand picks through it and cleans.

Believe me, you're going to find this information very helpful.

Every evening, the gibbons return to their home tree and groom each other again—the same way. Sometimes they have sex. You've always wondered how gibbons have sex, haven't you? Well, haven't we all? Here are the titillating details.

The male gibbon swings past his woman on a branch several times to indicate his interest. Taking his cue without hesitation, the female quickly assumes the position. She never complains of a headache. She never tries to get away from him. You see, ladies, what we can learn from the animal kingdom?

The male hangs from a branch and quickly completes the act while swinging back and forth like a pendulum. I told you this would be exciting. Near the end of the sexual act, the female cries out these phrases in her gibbon language: "Oh, honey! Yes, yes! You are the biggest gibbon stud in the forest!"

Okay, I'm just kidding about these phrases.

In fact, there is *no* passion. Just the mechanical act. The gibbons have sex exactly this same way every time.

At the end of the evening, they hold each other in the manner they always do and go to sleep.

The married gibbon couple performs these same carefully programmed rituals day in and day out for years—until one of them dies.

What the Gibbons Teach Us About Marriage

Why have I described for you the daily life of the gibbon couple?

What can we learn from the gibbons? Am I going to recommend that you sing together in the front yard of your home for two hours every morning? No. It might be fun, but no one has the time. Besides, the neighborhood SWAT team—I mean, the community association board—would send you a nasty letter.

Am I going to recommend that you have sex like the gibbons, with the male swinging in on a branch? Yes. Yes, I am. This is the secret to a happy marriage. Actually, no. You could try it, but that's not what I have in mind.

We can learn from the gibbons that we, as human married couples, are just like them. We perform rituals, rigid patterned behaviors, day in and day out for years.

By describing the gibbons and their daily behaviors, I have described the typical human married couple. I may have come dangerously close to describing your relationship.

The Rituals of the Typical Married Couple

Let's take a close look at the typical married couple. After a few years together, they have settled into a basic, unchanging daily routine.

I could set my watch by their rituals. He's getting the morning paper...now. He's finishing his dinner and belching...now. He's turning on the television and tuning her out...now. She's trying to tell him about her day and getting no response...now. She's calling her mother and seven friends on the phone...now.

This couple does the same old things in the morning. They repeat the same lines at the breakfast table:

Wife:	" 'Morning, honey."
Husband:	" 'Morning, honey."
Wife:	"It's gonna be a hot one."
Husband:	"Yeah, feels like it."
Wife:	"Looks like rain."
Husband:	"Sure does."
Wife:	"Have a nice day."

Husband:	"You too."
Wife:	"See you tonight."
Husband:	"Okay."

As they part in the morning, they engage in their time-honored ritual of the goodbye peck. Their lips, thinned out to hard nubs, touch for the briefest of instants. No moisture. No open mouths. No warmth. No lingering of any kind. No fun either. But that's the way they kiss goodbye. They do it the same way every morning.

This gibbon—I mean, human—couple does the same old things every evening. She's working on dinner and getting started on some household chores. He's sitting in front of the computer. She's helping the kids with their homework and getting them off to bed. He's got the television on and is zipping through the channels with his remote. She's on the phone with a friend or reading a novel. They practice the same basic routine every evening.

They do the same old things every weekend. Do yard work. Wash the cars. Cart the kids to sporting events and birthday parties. Go to the mall. Go to the grocery store. Play with the kids. Visit the grandparents. Watch sports on television. Go to church. Very little variation.

This couple performs these rituals over and over and over. Day in and day out. Week in and week out. Month in and month out. Year in and year out. They're used to the rituals. They're familiar. They're comfortable. And they're boring. Mind-numbingly tedious. No surprises. No spontaneity. No intimacy. No passion.

The Same Old Communication Script

This couple communicates, or doesn't communicate, the same way every day. They use the same lines they've used for years! They act as if they're following the script of a bad soap opera episode.

The wife tries to get the husband to open up and share something personal. She wants to stir up a little conversation. She wants to find out what's going on in his heart and mind. She wants to create some closeness. And so she asks the question she's asked every day for years: "How was your day?"

Reading from his script, he gives one of the five responses he always gives:

"Fine."
"Okay."
"All right."
"So-so."
"The usual."

These male human responses are designed to provide zero information to the female human and to shut down the conversation. And that's exactly what they do. This is all part of the daily communication ritual.

The ritual usually continues with the wife making more attempts to develop some dialogue with her mate. I think you'll recognize these female conversational approaches and the male responses:

Wife: "Did anything interesting happen today?"
Husband: "No."
"Not really."
"I like to leave work at work."
Wife: "What's on your mind?"
Husband: "Nothing."
Wife: "What are you thinking about right now?"
Husband: "Nothing."
Wife: (any question probing for personal information)
Husband: "I don't know."
"I don't want to talk about it."
(No response—he says nothing at all.)
"Please, honey, not now; let's talk about that later." (Of course, later never comes).

After hitting a dead end with her questions, the wife will go to the next stage of the ritual. She'll share her own personal information about her day and life experiences. She's hoping he'll respond with interest and join her in the conversation. Of course, that doesn't happen. The husband faithfully follows his part of the ritual: He gives no response, acts distracted and fidgety, asks her to stop rambling and to cut to the chase, and finally tunes her out and stops listening altogether. She catches him not listening and gets angry and hurt. Any hope for real intimacy has been killed again.

In another key part of the communication ritual, the wife describes a problem she's facing with a coworker, family member, child, fellow church member, or friend. She wants her husband to listen, understand her feelings, show concern for what she's going through, and walk in her shoes. But that's not his script in this ritual.

He uses logic and tries to fix her problem. He plays devil's advocate and tries to help her see the other person's point of view. He says incredibly unhelpful things:

> "Those things happen."
>
> "I have days like that—get used to it."
>
> "Just suck it up and go on."
>
> "Relax, don't let it bother you."
>
> "Get a grip."
>
> "If you don't like your job, why don't you just quit?"

The Same Old Conflict Script

When they get angry with each other, this couple automatically moves into their "here's how we deal with conflict" ritual. They act out the same behaviors and deliver the same words every single time. And every single time, they get the same results: an unresolved conflict, simmering resentments, and a relationship that is a little colder and more distant. Check out these classic conflict rituals:

She says those four words that strike terror in his heart: "We need to talk." His throat tightens, and his bowels begin to loosen. Inside, he recoils as if she just said, "I'm going to tie you to a chair and torture you until you scream with pain." He immediately goes into his avoidance routine. He says nothing as she talks. He does not make eye contact. He refuses to engage. He will not respond. After ten or fifteen minutes of trying, she stops and goes to her room. She's angry, hurt, and completely frustrated.

Or after listening to her express her feelings and point of view for several minutes, he calmly interrupts and informs her she has it completely wrong. Totally ignoring her feelings, he "corrects" them. After all, doesn't he know better than she does how she feels? He proceeds to tell her in a rational, unemotional manner what actually happened. She is overpowered by his articulate, logical, and persuasive presentation. She can't compete with him verbally, so she gives in.

Both spouses escalate quickly in the conflict. Both are shouting. Both are interrupting. Neither is listening. Suddenly, the man has had enough and walks away. The woman becomes even angrier and follows him, continuing to make her case in a loud, sarcastic way. He locks himself in the bedroom or drives off in his car.

The husband and wife throw the same old phrases at each other in every conflict:

> "Do we have to talk about this now?"
>
> "You're too emotional."
>
> "Don't use that tone with me."
>
> "I didn't say that!"
>
> "That's not what happened!"
>
> "You're just like your mother."
>
> "Listen to me!"
>
> "Are you through yet?"
>
> "That's not worth being upset about."
>
> "Talk to me; say something!"
>
> "Don't walk away!"

The Same Old Sex Script

It's time for the typical married couple to make love. Will it be a spontaneous, playful, and unpredictable experience? No. No, it won't be. They will make love the same way they always do. Just like a synchronized swimming team, they'll go through the same motions. From his pinch on her bottom signaling it's her lucky night to her pat on his back when it's all over, every move and every word is carefully choreographed.

Sex is about as thrilling as washing the car or cleaning the bathrooms. It doesn't make any difference if you do those chores the same way every time. But it makes a huge difference if you follow the identical sexual routine every time. Boring. Boring. Boring.

I've heard thousands of married couples in my therapy office describe their stale, predictable sex lives. I ask them, "Why don't you just videotape your sex and then just watch the tape from then on? That would be about as exciting as the real thing."

Your Rituals Are Killing Your Marriage

Now you tell me. What is the difference between this human couple and a gibbon couple? There is no difference. They're the same! So don't laugh at the gibbons. You and your spouse *are* the gibbons! If I took two gibbons from southeastern Asia and moved them in next door to you and your mate, you couldn't tell the difference.

With one exception.

The gibbons' rituals don't kill their passion. They don't have any passion—they're animals! The gibbons can go 40 or 50 years with their rituals and never get bored or lose intimacy. They're not unhappy. There aren't any gibbon marriage counselors. Observers have not recorded a single incident of a gibbon getting tired of marriage and leaving. Monkey experts have studied this in the forest.

The rituals *do* kill the passion of us human couples. Doing the same things and saying the same things the same way kills our passion, and the process doesn't take very long. Husbands and wives say to me, "We fell out of love," or "Sometimes love just dies."

I say, "Baloney. Love has to be killed, and your rituals killed it. You ought to go to prison for killing your marriage. It's marriage slaughter. You didn't mean to. It wasn't premeditated. But you killed it."

Slavishly following your rituals is like eating a cheeseburger with onion and mustard at every meal. Cheeseburger at breakfast. Cheeseburger at lunch. Cheeseburger at dinner. And doing it for months and years. After a while, a cheeseburger is nauseating. The pleasure and passion are gone. You know exactly how it will taste.

You want to eat something different, something new, but you don't know how. The cheeseburger is all you've ever known, so you keep eating it. You won't die of starvation, but you'll wish you were dead.

And Now, Something Completely Different

The same lines. The same approaches to conversation. The same attempts at intimacy. The same defensive maneuvers to avoid closeness. The same daily behaviors. The same kisses. The same routines. The same married life every day. You're boring each other to death!

Enough is enough!

It's time to do something new in your relationship, isn't it? It's time to break the old patterns, get rid of the old rituals, and start fresh. It's time to build a marriage that really works—for both of you.

I can't help the gibbons. But I can help you. To stop your relationship rituals, you need to know what causes them.

I know what causes the rituals.

Marriage Enrichment Steps

1. Talk about your rituals as a married couple. What do you do over and over in the morning, in the evening, and on weekends?

2. What are your communication rituals? How does the wife try to get conversation going, and how does the husband respond? To which parts of the communication script can each of you relate?

3. How do you deal with conflict? What is your conflict ritual? Which classic conflict ritual most closely resembles how you two handle arguments?

4. Are you doing sex the same old way every time? How is your love life these days?

5. Agree that you're both going to stop your rituals and start fresh. Pray—right now—that God will help you build a new marriage.

2

Cinderella and the Caveman
Make a Deal

The Most Popular—and Deadly—Marriage Contract

All romantic relationships begin with a contract—an unwritten, unspoken, never-discussed agreement that creates roles and rituals for the partners to follow. This contract eventually kills intimacy.

Every married couple has a contract. And just about every couple I've ever known—friends, family, neighbors, the thousands of couples I've worked with in therapy in the past 20 years, and the thousands more I've talked to at my marriage seminars across the United States—have the *same* contract.

My wife, Sandy, and I had this contract. I'll bet you and your spouse had it and probably may still have it. What's it called?

Cinderella Meets the Caveman

This contract determines how we will live together. It creates specific, rigid roles for us to play. The roles—Cinderella and the Caveman—lead to the rituals. It leaves no room for spontaneity, no room for creativity.

Each of us has a script we follow. Wives follow the Cinderella script, and husbands follow the Caveman script. These scripts apply to every situation, every time of day, every interaction, every conversation, every conflict, and every sexual encounter.

The Cinderella and Caveman scripts—and the rituals that go with them—kill every single opportunity for intimacy. Most couples never achieve intimacy because these scripts create a predictable, boring relationship. Intimacy is always unpredictable and spontaneous, but the rituals embedded in the scripts make us do the same old things the same old ways.

The scripts also kill intimacy by preventing emotional and spiritual connection. The rituals are mistakes—intimacy-killing mistakes—that keep Cinderella and the Caveman at a distance and rob them of the heart-and-soul connection they each desperately need.

Are you ready for a description of Cinderella and the Caveman? Good. Here we go. I think their scripts will sound familiar.

Meet Cinderella

You know the story. Cinderella's father, a wealthy and kind man, is a widower. He treats Cinderella like a princess, and they are very happy together. But the poor man is lonely, so he marries a woman with two daughters of her own. The nice but somewhat clueless man is duped by his new wife into believing she is a wonderful person who will love both him and Cinderella. Unfortunately, she turns out to be an absolute witch.

After Cinderella's father dies suddenly, she is left at the mercy of the stepmother from hell. This horribly cruel, evil woman makes Cinderella a slave in her own home. She and her vain, selfish, and equally cruel daughters live in idle comfort while Cinderella does all the work in the home.

All day long, every day, Cinderella works herself to death. She makes the meals, does the dishes, washes the clothes, scrubs the floors, cleans the drapes, feeds the pets, and meets every need of these three female monsters. Why does she work so hard? She doesn't have to. She has other options. Why not just leave? Her life couldn't be worse anywhere else! But not in this story. This is her script, and she follows it.

Cinderella allows all kinds of horrific mistreatment by her abusive stepmother and two vicious stepsisters. They heap neglect, rejection, physical abuse, emotional abuse, and humiliation on her every day of her miserable life. Why doesn't she do something to protect herself and build a better life? It's part of her role, that's why.

Cinderella slaves away for years, passively and meekly accepting her role as slave and abused peasant girl. The only thing that keeps her going is her one great dream: One day, out of the clear blue, the prince will come for her and take her to his castle. She fantasizes obsessively about how the prince will rescue her, sweep her off her feet, and love her forever.

She keeps this dream a secret. She never breathes a word about it to anyone. At least not to any human. She makes no attempt to make the dream happen. She doesn't write a letter to the prince. She doesn't try to meet him. She doesn't try to get a job in the castle so she might come into contact with him.

She just expects the prince to somehow find her and make her happy. She only speaks about him with the animals and birds. But obviously, they can't help her.

When Cinderella finally gets her chance to meet the prince and dance with him, she absolutely blows it! She doesn't give him her address. She doesn't give him her phone number. She doesn't even give him her name! She runs off at midnight, leaving only her glass slipper behind. And even that was an accident!

In this crazy story, through magic and a set of bizarre and unbelievable circumstances, Cinderella ends up with the prince. Amazing!

Three of our kids are girls—Emily, Leeann, and Nancy—and they loved this story when they were little. I read the various book versions to them countless times. I watched the different movie adaptations with them over and over and over.

Trying to be a good dad and provide some helpful teaching, I challenged the irrational, unhealthy aspects of the Cinderella story. Here's what I said to my little girls:

> "Why does Cinderella take all that terrible abuse?"
>
> "Why does she keep on serving these three persons who hate her and treat her like a dog?"

"Girls, don't ever be as pathetically subassertive and dependent as Cinderella."

"Come on, Cinderella, get a backbone and speak up!"

"She ought to drop that breakfast tray right into her ugly stepmother's lap. Back then, you couldn't sue if you got burned by hot tea or coffee."

"Cinderella, now that you're actually dancing with the man of your dreams, open your silly mouth and tell him who you are and where you live! Slip him a note!"

"Use American Sign Language! Tell him you're trapped in an abusive home!"

"He's a prince, you dummy! He can ride in with his soldiers and rescue you!"

My girls didn't appreciate my input. They'd say, "Daddy, be quiet! Don't make fun of Cinderella! It all works out in the end." My dear wife, Sandy, would tell me—in a nice way—to shut up and stop ruining it for the girls.

My tongue-in-cheek comments to the girls were designed to be humorous. But I also was genuinely concerned about the unhealthy way Cinderella lived her life. I did not want my girls to be like her.

In the real world, we can't depend on magic. In the real world, Cinderella would never get her prince, and she would stay miserable. And she should! Why? Because she's not willing to do anything constructive to change her situation! Cinderella is certainly a hard-working young woman, but her efforts are misguided. She desperately wants her dream of being close to the prince to come true, but she takes the wrong approach to getting it.

The Cinderella Mind-Set

Look, I know the story of Cinderella is fiction. It's a fairy tale. But it illustrates how most wives think, feel, and act in their marriages. This Cinderella mind-set denies them the intimacy with their husbands they desire and need.

The Cinderella wife not only tries too hard to get close to her husband, she also tries in the same old ineffective ways. And she often allows her husband and others to mistreat her.

But her central and most critical mistake is that she lives in an idealistic, romantic world, where she strongly believes her husband ought to instinctively understand and meet her needs. I have heard these statements from thousands of wives:

"Without me having to say a word, my man should just know what my needs are."

"It's true love if my man figures out my heart's desire on his own and sweeps me off my feet."

"Everything's spoiled if I have to tell him my needs! All he has to do is pay attention! If he really cared, he'd just know!"

This Cinderella mind-set, particularly in the area of communicating needs, happens in conversations between wives and husbands all the time.

Woman: (She's at home and calls the man at work.) "Honey, I feel really sick and shaky all over. I don't know if I can make it through the day."

Man: "I'm sorry, honey. Look, just relax and take it easy. Call the doctor if you need to. I'll see you tonight."

Woman: "Thanks for nothing! I ask for some help and get the big kiss-off! You don't care about me, do you?"

Man: "I do care. I love you. What can I do for you? What do you want?"

Woman: "Oh, never mind. I'll make it." (Hangs up.)

The man is thinking, *What did I do wrong?* He hears the musical theme from *The Twilight Zone*. Actually, it's the Cinderella Zone.

Here's what happened: The woman expected the man to come home and be with her. She thought she sent that message and he deliberately ignored it.

No! He never got that message! She didn't tell him what she wanted!

Another woman would have heard, "Come home, please," but not a man. Men are not intuitive. We miss the hidden message! If you want your husband to come home, you have to tell him. "Please come home. I need you here."

Let's listen to the same married couple a few weeks later. It's Thursday evening, and they are sitting on the couch in the living room.

> Woman: (She's missing the man and wants some time with him.) "Boy, this has been a busy week. We haven't had much time together." (Hint, hint. She's dying for him to say, "You want some time with me, don't you? How about we spend some time right now talking, and I'll also take you out Friday night on a date. I've missed you too." Is that what he says? Are you kidding?)

> Man: "Yeah, it has been busy. Sure has. Some weeks are like that."

> Woman: (She's disappointed and a little irritated. He didn't get the message. He didn't respond the way she wanted. She tries again with a little edge to her voice.) "Have you really missed something this week, something important?" (She's talking about herself! It's so obvious to her what she means. But not to him. Like a cow being led to the slaughter, the man doesn't pick up the difference in her voice. He doesn't realize this is his last chance to get it.)

> Man: "Let me see. Yeah, honey, there were a few things I really missed. I missed seeing the football game on television, and I missed the chance to clean the garage. That shows how busy I was."

Woman:	(She's angry and hurt.) "Well, it's nice to know that a football game and the garage are more important to you than I am!"
Man:	(He now knows he's in trouble, but he doesn't know why or how it happened.) "Huh? What are you so angry about? You asked me what I missed this week, and I told you."
Woman:	"Exactly. I wanted to know if you missed *me*—you know, your wife—this week!"
Man:	"Oh, well, sure I missed you." (The light has dawned, but it's too little, too late for this poor sucker. It's gonna be a long night as he tries to convince the woman he does love her and he did miss her.)

Cinderella thinks she made it crystal clear that she wanted personal time with him. She didn't! She didn't say that! All he heard is that they've been busy and haven't had much time together.

He does not make the leap to the real message of her wanting time with him and wanting to know if he missed her. Most men can't make that leap.

It's a special code you Cinderellas have. Men don't know the code!

Maybe, just maybe, a very sensitive man could decipher your code and come through for you in a miraculous way. But you didn't marry a sensitive man. You married the Caveman.

Meet the Caveman

Unlike Cinderella, who thinks of everyone but herself, the Caveman thinks only about himself. When the Caveman marries Cinderella, it's a perfect match. She thinks about him and his needs, and he thinks about him and his needs. What could be better?

The Caveman figures, *Hey, we agree on the most important thing… my needs!* All the Caveman asks is that his woman meet his three basic needs.

His first need is for food. Most men live with the constant fear of not getting enough to eat. A man who eats well is a happy man. You've heard the saying, "The way to a man's heart is through his stomach." Not really. It pretty much begins and ends in his stomach. When a man is full, he won't give you his heart. Just a belch and his empty plate.

The Caveman's second critical need is clothing. The woman's job (of course, everything is the woman's job) is to make sure the man's clothes are clean and put away in the proper place. This is in the United States Constitution. Even the Founding Fathers knew our country could not survive unless the women meet the men's clothing needs.

It is nothing short of a catastrophe—second only to the woman having no clear plan for dinner—if the Caveman cannot find a particular article of clothing when he needs it.

Here's a case in point. All day long, like most days, the wife has done things for her husband: She prepared his breakfast, got the kids ready and off to school, worked at her own job, cleaned the home, went grocery shopping, cooked dinner, put the kids to bed, and listened to him talk about his day.

Late in the evening, the man lays out his clothes for the next day. He opens his sock drawer and freezes. Gasp! He can't believe his shocked eyes! He doesn't have any clean socks!

We know what happens at this point, don't we? He goes to his wife and gently says, "Honey, you've done so much for me today. I'm embarrassed to even bring this up. I don't seem to have any socks in my drawer. How can we solve this situation?"

Is that what he does? Not even close! The very second he sees no socks, he yells, "I don't have any socks in my drawer!" Panic and exasperation fill his voice. This is a serious crisis situation. His life, his whole career, teeters in the balance!

Then he grouses around the home, mumbling to himself. "I don't ask for much around here. Just to have a few clean socks in my drawer." If he's smart, he doesn't mumble this loud enough for the woman to hear him.

What kind of a selfish ingrate would have the nerve to complain about socks when the woman has done ten thousand other things for him that day? I'll tell you who. Me! I've pulled this kind of stunt many times. I'm not proud of it. It's a Caveman thing I have to fight.

The Caveman's final need will come as a total shock to you ladies. Brace yourselves. It's sex. Not too shocking, is it? You knew this would be on the list, didn't you?

Women, you must understand the terrible truth about your man and sex. He thinks about sex once every seven seconds. He spends the other six seconds wondering why he's not thinking about sex. When he wants sex, it becomes an obsession. It's all he can think about. Whatever you are doing and however you are feeling makes no difference to him. He thinks, *Hey, you get to have sex with me. Isn't that enough for you?* Pitiful, isn't it?

When he feels the urge for sex—and it can strike without warning at any time of the day or night—he needs to have it as quickly as possible. In fact, if he can't have sex within 30 minutes, something bad will happen. He'll break out in a terrible rash. He'll start shaking uncontrollably. He'll be emotionally scarred. He'll be physically damaged. He could explode because of the awesome pressure building up in his body. He could actually die! You don't want to kill this poor man, do you?

Actually, this isn't true. It takes 45 minutes for these bad things to happen.

The real truth is that no man ever died or was permanently harmed from sex being delayed. This attitude toward sex is part of the Caveman mentality that is embedded in most of us men.

The Caveman Mind-Set

These examples provide a clear picture of how the vast majority of husbands think, feel, and act in their marriages. This Caveman mind-set robs a husband of closeness, denies him the respect and attention he craves, and deeply wounds the woman he loves.

The central, core weakness of the Caveman is his selfishness. It's all about him: The Caveman lives in a self-centered, logical world where he expects his wife to meet his needs on demand. He is a master at avoiding intimacy. He actually has a deep need for intimacy but doesn't realize it. Because of his insensitivity and ignorance of his wife's needs, he unwittingly mistreats her over and over again.

The Origins of Cinderella and the Caveman

Neither partner is being malicious. No one is trying intentionally to cause hurt and kill intimacy. The husband and wife are simply acting out roles that are determined by DNA and sex-role training.

These roles are born *and* made. Women are born Cinderellas and men are born Cavemen. It's genetic. God made us this way. The Cinderella and Cavemen mind-sets and the mistakes that result come naturally. They're automatic, unconscious. They're just what we do.

Also, and very importantly, our parents and others we were close to in childhood provided an early and intensely influential education in these roles. Moms and other women teach little girls how to be Cinderellas. Dads and other men teach little boys how to be Cavemen.

In about 10 to 15 percent of marriages, these roles are reversed. The husband acts out the Cinderella role and the wife acts out the Caveman role. This is perfectly normal. The principles in the following chapters will still apply and help you. Just reverse the sexes.

The Road to Intimacy

Breaking out of these roles is difficult, but you must do it, or you'll be stuck with a mediocre marriage at best. Mediocre marriages become miserable marriages. Miserable marriages don't glorify God, they drain all the life and joy out of both partners, and they often end in divorce.

There is a way out. A way to revive your marriage. Perhaps, to bring it back from the dead. To get out of the boring rut you've been in. To be joyful. To be closer than you've ever been. To be passionate. To enjoy great sex.

If you're okay with a boring, mediocre marriage (or worse), put this book back on the shelf or give it to a friend. If you want a terrific marriage, you've got the right book in your hands. Here's the road map we'll follow.

In part 1, I explain how you built a boring marriage. You did it the same way almost all couples do. You acted out the rituals in the original Cinderella Meets the Caveman contract.

In part 2, I expose the five major mistakes Cinderella and the Caveman make and, I show how to correct them. Cinderella speaks in code and doesn't make her needs clear, she pursues her husband too intensely, she's too focused on the children and the home, she allows her husband to mistreat her, and she is not a good sexual partner. The Caveman is selfish, he resists intimacy, he's not connected to his children, he unintentionally mistreats his wife, and he fails to romance his wife.

In part 3, I show you how to fight. If you can't fight effectively and work through conflicts, you can't get anywhere near intimacy. I help you identify your dysfunctional conflict pattern—every couple has one—and describe a conflict resolution strategy that works.

Finally, in part 4, I describe how to start over in your marriage by attacking your rituals, peeling off your intimacy substitutes, creating a spiritual bond, and learning to fire up your sex life.

If your spouse won't read this book—and some won't—that's okay. You'll read it, you'll change, and your marriage will change.

I need to warn you right up front that I will be hard on both wives and husbands. You each will take your turns in the hot seat. I won't pull any punches. I'll be direct, honest, and blunt. That's how I do therapy, and that's how I write. That's the approach I needed—and still need. You need the truth, or you won't change. I don't mean to offend, although at times I will. I mean to get your attention, motivate you to act differently, and show you how—with God's help—to build the marriage you want and God desires you to have.

Marriage Enrichment Steps

1. Wife, do you like the story of Cinderella? Tell your husband why you like it. What makes it appeal to you?

2. Wife, can you relate to the Cinderella mind-set of expecting your husband to know your needs without making them clear to him? Why do you think you use the special code?

3. Husband, can you relate to the Caveman mind-set of being selfish? Can you admit that, most of the time, you think of yourself and your needs first? Why do you think you do this?

4. Agree now, as husband and wife, that you will...

   - read the chapters that deal with your mistakes,

   - discuss together the marriage enrichment steps, and

   - work hard to correct your mistakes.

   Seal this commitment right now with a prayer together.

Part Two

How to Correct the Cinderella and Caveman Mistakes

3

Cinderella, You're Speaking in Code

Be Clear About Your Needs

I've talked to thousands of men in my therapy office and in my seminars, and I've heard all their complaints about their wives. One of their biggest beefs is the way wives talk in code. I've heard the same message from these frustrated husbands over and over: "Doc, I love my wife, but I can't seem to please her! I try to do things for her, but I end up being wrong most of the time. I want to make her happy, but I don't know how."

When I've spoken to the wives of these men, here's what they've told me: "My husband knows exactly what my needs are, and he simply chooses not to meet them. I feel angry and hurt, and I feel like he doesn't love me very much."

This is my response to these wives: "Your original assumption is incorrect. Believe me, he couldn't name your needs if his life depended on it. He's a Caveman. I'll work with him on that.

"But also, he doesn't know your needs because you don't tell him your needs in a way he can understand. Your Caveman doesn't meet many of your needs because you don't communicate them clearly. You think you do, but you don't."

Cinderella, you use a special language to communicate your needs to your Caveman. Unfortunately, he has no idea how to crack this code. The answer for you is not to hope and pray he can figure out your code. You won't live that long. The answer for you is to correct the three Cinderella code mistakes and learn to express clearly your needs.

CINDERELLA CODE MISTAKE 1

Saying Nothing at All and Expecting Your Caveman to Meet Your Needs

Like most wives, you assume that your Caveman knows exactly what your needs are and that he simply chooses not to meet them. Without giving him any clues he can decipher, you expect him to somehow figure out what you need and come through for you. You think, *If he really loved me, he'd know just what I need.*

I think you're living in a fantasy world and being unrealistic and unfair to your husband.

The truth is, your Caveman has no idea what your needs are. Here's a man who can't find his shoes in the morning. A man who is about as sensitive and intuitive as a marble paperweight. A man who doesn't even know what *his* real needs are. How in the world do you expect him—on his own—to identify and meet your needs?

Don't Be Terry McKay

A good example of a Cinderella who says nothing about her needs is Deborah Kerr's character, Terry McKay, in the famous chick flick, *An Affair to Remember.* Terry and Cary Grant's character, Nickie Ferrante, fall deeply and desperately in love on an ocean liner. They're perfect for each other. Soul mates. The only catch is that they are each engaged to someone else. They plan to meet in six months at the top of the Empire State Building if they still feel the same way about each other.

Terry is on her way to their rendezvous—she's right across the street—when she's hit by a car and seriously injured. Poor Nickie waits for hours and hours and finally has to leave because the observation deck is closing. He's forced to assume that she has changed her mind and doesn't want to be his wife.

Terry's legs are crippled in the accident, and she may never walk again. When she wakes up in the hospital after surgery, she immediately gets word to Nickie to come to her. He rushes to her bedside, and she explains what happened. Nickie holds her and assures her he loves her and wants to marry her, crippled legs and all. They get married and are very happy.

Is this what happens in the movie? Of course not! It's what should have happened, but if you've seen the movie you know what Terry chooses to do. In classic Cinderella fashion, she says absolutely nothing to Nickie. No call. No note. No message through a friend. Absolutely no communication.

Nickie is in agony. His life is ruined. The woman he dearly loves didn't show up for their romantic meeting, and he has no idea why. Terry decides that because she's now crippled, she doesn't want to burden Nickie. She thinks he wouldn't want her. So she says nothing and disappears from his life. The nerve! The unmitigated gall!

Why does she fail to give Nickie the option of deciding for himself? What kind of weird thinking is this? Did the accident cause brain damage? No. Terry is making the Cinderella mistake of saying nothing and expecting the Caveman to meet her needs. How can he show her his love when she won't even tell him the truth about the accident? She still loves him and wants him, but she will say nothing to help the poor guy find her and pledge his love.

Nickie stumbles across Terry at the end of the movie. As they talk awkwardly in her apartment, she reclines on the couch with a blanket over her crippled legs. Incredibly, she still says nothing to Nickie! He finally figures it out on his own and tenderly tells her he doesn't care in the least if she's crippled.

He should have said, "You're not only a cripple, you're a liar!" and walked out on her. But of course, that wouldn't be a Hollywood ending. She puts him through unimaginable torment for months because she refused to tell him the truth about her accident.

Sandy and the Laundry

My wife, Sandy, has been just as guilty as you and Terry of the mistake of saying nothing about needs. Here's just one example. Until recently, Sandy would start a load of laundry on a Saturday afternoon. She'd get the washer going in the garage and then come into the house to tell me she was going shopping for a while. I'd say, "Great, honey. Have a good time." She'd say, "Thanks. I will. See you later."

Sandy would leave and expect me to finish that load of laundry. The only problem was, I had *no idea* she had clothes in the washer! How could I know that? She never said a word about it! Unless I happened to wander into the garage and hear the washer, I'd never know.

Sandy would come back home and say to me in a sarcastic tone, "Hey, thanks a lot for finishing the laundry for me." I'd ask, with a completely straight face, "What laundry?" Sandy (I'm not kidding here) would actually think that I knew about the load of laundry and that I had selfishly ignored it! Women! Cinderellas!

I have finally convinced Sandy that she has to tell me about the laundry before she leaves if she expects me to finish it for her. Like most husbands, I'd be happy to meet a need as long as I know what it is. If Sandy doesn't tell me her needs, that's her fault, not mine.

I do try to focus on Sandy and anticipate some of her needs. If she does leave the house on Saturday without mentioning the laundry, I still run to the garage to check the washer. Sometimes, a load is going, and I can surprise her by finishing it. Meeting one of her needs without her saying a word is fun. But that is a rare occurrence. The old saying, "Even a blind squirrel finds a few acorns" comes to mind. You can't build a great, need-meeting marriage on those few times a year when a husband stumbles onto an unspoken need and meets it.

CINDERELLA CODE MISTAKE 2

Sending a Message About Your Needs That Your Caveman Cannot Understand

Sometimes the woman has told the man what she wants him to do. At least she thinks she's told him. She actually believes she sent a crystal-clear message that only an insensitive, uncaring lout could miss. The man does miss it, but not because he's a brute. She happened to send the message in her female code. When he fails to meet her need, she's upset. She's convinced it's his fault! He's in trouble, and he doesn't even know why.

I Want to Go to the Craft Class

Check out this true story that I heard recently in my therapy office.

A wife gets off the phone and says to her husband, "That was my friend Susie. I haven't talked to her for a while. She's going to a craft class this Saturday morning. I'll bet that's going to be fun. I used to do crafts all the time." She thinks she said, "Susie's going to the craft class, and I want to go with her. I miss her and want to renew our friendship. Even though I enjoy crafts, it's not really about crafts. It's about our relationship. She's reaching out to me, and that feels good. Is it okay with you if I go?"

She didn't say what she thinks she said! Now, another woman would have immediately gotten her real message. But she married a man. Her husband doesn't get the message because she never sent the message. At least not in language he can understand.

Come Saturday morning, she's an emotional wreck because she's been waiting for him to discuss the craft class with her. He has no idea what's going on. He's completely forgotten about the class! An ugly scene develops as she pours out her pain to him.

She assumes he realizes she wants to go to the craft class so she can spend time with her friend. She goes into a 20-minute monologue about how little time she has for friends. One time—one lousy time—she has a chance to be with a friend, and he denies her the opportunity. Her assumption that he got her message is incorrect! She's built up all these painful feelings out of thin air.

Is this fair? No! Is it the way most wives operate? You'd better believe it. Cinderella incorrectly assumes she sends a clear message to her Caveman. Then, when he does nothing, she builds a whole scenario in her mind about what a crumb he is. *He's this and he's that. He feels this way or that way about me. He has the nerve to… He is such a…*

This wife was shocked out of her head when I told her she was the one who blew it in this situation. She was sure I'd confront her husband for not acting on her clear message. She was wrong. I informed her in my gentle, diplomatic way that she was guilty of using the Cinderella code and that no man on earth would have understood her message.

CINDERELLA CODE MISTAKE 3

Getting Upset with Your Caveman and Refusing to Tell Him Why

Here is a marital scene that is repeated millions of times a day in homes across the globe.

The woman and the man are together at home, and the woman is in a funk. She's quiet, withdrawn—just not herself. The man, after a while, notices that she's upset.

Caveman: "What's wrong, honey?"

Cinderella: "You know what's wrong."

Caveman: "No, I don't know what's wrong. That's why I asked."

Cinderella: "Oh, you know all right. Don't play dumb with me. I know you know."

Caveman: (He searches his small brain. *What could it be? What have I done this time?* He comes up empty.) "I really don't know. I have no idea."

Cinderella: (She is insulted and angry.) "Well, if you don't know, I'm certainly not going to tell you!"

Caveman: (He is bewildered and flabbergasted.) "Honey, wait a minute. Be reasonable. I don't know, so you need to tell me. Then we'll both know, and we can have a normal conversation. Who knows, maybe I can help you feel better."

Sound familiar? The Caveman can't win. Even when Cinderella

eventually tells him what's bothering her, she's unhappy because he should have known in the first place. And by the time she tells him, she's worked up quite an emotional lather of anger and hurt.

Cinderella, can you see what's happening here? You don't clearly tell your Caveman what you need in the first place. He doesn't come through, so you're upset. But you don't tell him why because he ought to know. He doesn't know what has happened! He doesn't know what your original need was, and he doesn't know why you're so offended now.

Whose fault is this? It's *your* fault, Cinderella. Your unbreakable code has created confusion and pain. Without realizing it, you're making yourself and your Caveman miserable. Maybe you can relate to some of the justifications that follow.

The Dialogue

Cinderella: "We live together in the same home! How can he not see my needs? They're obvious!"

Me: "No, your needs are not obvious. They would be to a woman, but you didn't marry a woman. You married a Caveman. He's dense, and he's not a special case. Ninety-nine percent of men are like this. I'm a clinical psychologist, and I'm the same way."

Cinderella: "He should know me and love me enough to figure out my needs."

Me: "That's magical thinking. Stop it. He does know you and he does love you, but that doesn't mean he can figure out your needs on his own."

Cinderella: "Telling him spoils everything. If I state a need clearly, I'm not sure he really wants to do it. Is he meeting my need because he has to, or is it really the desire of his heart?"

Me: "Not telling him spoils everything. Go ahead

and tell him, or he won't know. His response and attitude after you share the need will tell you if he's being sincere."

Cinderella: "I don't want to seem too demanding. I don't want to burden him with my needs."

Me: "According to the Bible, meeting your needs is his job. But if you don't tell him what they are, he can't meet them. Then you'll resent him and be angry and pull back emotionally and physically. That behavior will put an unfair burden on him."

State Your Needs Clearly to Your Caveman

Your Caveman requires the conversational equivalent of a brick to the head. Saying nothing won't work. Sending a coded message won't work. Getting upset and thinking he ought to know why won't work. The only thing that will work is to tell the man in clear, direct words exactly what you need and exactly when you want the behavior accomplished.

Make sure you have his attention. A Caveman cannot do two things at once. Don't be vague. Don't hint. Don't be coy. Don't be subtle. Use plain English. Be brief. Be specific.

Terry McKay: "Look, I was hit by a car on the way to our meeting. My legs are crippled. I still love you and want you, but I'm not sure how you'll feel about me with my physical limitations. Come to the hospital, and let's talk about our relationship."

Sandy: "I've started a load of laundry. Please finish it, fold the clothes, and put them away."

Sit down with your Caveman and let him know you're sorry for not being clear with your needs. From now on, you'll be working hard to communicate in a clear, direct way what you need from him. Tell him you'll be sharing your needs both verbally and, at times, in writing.

Tell him that when you're expressing your needs in person, he has a choice: Would he rather write your needs down himself or have you hand him the list of needs you've written on a three-by-five card?

In this meeting about needs, you'll be explaining the four strategies I explain below. This is your good faith effort to get your Caveman on board with the new need-meeting program. Ask him for input, suggestions, and his ideas about how to meet your needs.

In the Morning and Throughout the Day

In the morning, before you go your separate ways, tell him verbally what you need him to do for you that day. He can jot down your needs, or you can hand him a three-by-five card with your needs listed on it. Tell him you would be thrilled if he completed these items by the end of the day.

> "Please call the plumber and have him come between 3:00 and 5:00."
>
> "Please pick up Johnny at 5:30."
>
> "Please get eggs, a gallon of milk, and angel hair pasta."
>
> "Please call your mother and tell her we can't make it Sunday."

If your needs change during the day, call or e-mail him to let him know.

> "I can't be home today for the plumber. Please schedule it for tomorrow."
>
> "Please add sour cream and tortilla chips to your grocery list."

When you see him in the early evening, tell him any additional needs you have for that night.

> "Honey, I need a ten-minute neck rub."
>
> "Please give Johnny a bath tonight."
>
> "Please cook the pasta while I handle the rest of the meal."

When you're sharing these needs in the early evening, you'll probably just do it verbally. However, if he forgets too often, use the writing approach. He can jot them down, or you can give him the three-by-five card.

I know what you're thinking: *I'm going to feel pretty dumb handing him a three-by-five card with my needs on it.* All I can say is that you'll feel a lot worse if your needs don't get met. Your Caveman has no memory, so a written list is often essential. I realize lovers in the movies don't use the need lists, but that's not real life!

Debrief and Prepare

In your 20- to 30-minute daily couple time (more on this in a later chapter), talk to him—with gentleness and respect—about how he handled your needs that day. Thank him for coming through and briefly express your feelings if he didn't meet certain needs.

If you know of specific needs you'll have for the next day, tell him. Men don't like surprises, so this will give him a heads-up. Again, he can jot them down or take your three-by-five card. In the morning, you can add to or subtract from the list of needs if necessary.

Post Your Needs for the Week

Sit down on Saturday or Sunday and make a list of your needs for the upcoming week. Use seven columns for the seven days. Under each day, list the needs you want met that day. Post this list of needs on the refrigerator so your husband can't miss it. You can make changes on the list as the week progresses. You'll still share your needs verbally and use the three-by-five card, but this is another effective way to communicate with your Caveman.

When He Doesn't Meet a Need

Obviously, your husband won't meet every need you express. But these communication strategies will significantly increase the percentage of met needs. When he fails to meet an important need and you're angry and hurt, you must go to him and briefly express your feelings in one-way communication. You will do all the talking, and you will ask him to listen and not respond at that time.

"Honey, I have something to say, and I just want you to listen and hear me out. Don't say anything. I'm angry and disappointed because you didn't call the plumber and you didn't get the groceries today. I was clear with those needs, and you didn't come through. I have to be honest so I can forgive you and not get resentful."

Say your piece and then walk away. This cleans your system and prevents bitterness and resentment from building up. Besides, your Caveman may respond to your honest expression and work harder to meet your needs. If he still has time, he may take action to meet the needs you just talked about.

Marriage Enrichment Steps

1. Do the three Cinderella code mistakes sound familiar? Tell your husband one recent example of how you did not make your needs clear to him.

2. Ask your husband to give you a recent example of how you did not make your needs clear to him.

3. What reasons or excuses do you use to avoid making your needs clear to your husband? What prevents you from being up-front and direct with your needs?

4. How did your mom share her needs with your dad? What did she teach you about sharing needs with a man?

5. Discuss with your husband the four need-meeting strategies. Which ones do you think will work for you as a couple?

6. Right now, give him a list of needs for tomorrow (verbally and in writing). Agree to meet tomorrow evening to talk about how the need-meeting practice went.

Caveman, You're Being Selfish

Focus on Her Needs

It's dark in the home. It ought to be. It's 1:00 a.m. The married couple is in bed, both sleeping soundly. Suddenly the man stirs and shakes the woman awake.

> Woman: "What...what is it?"
>
> Man: "I, uh, want to...uh, you know."
>
> Woman: "What are you talking about?"

Oh, she knows what he's talking about. She's just stalling for time, trying to get him off track. She harbors a very faint hope that maybe he'll realize the tacky, inappropriate, and absurd situation he's putting her in.

> Man: "You know, you and me. I feel like...being together. You know, making love."
>
> Woman: (She lights up immediately, gives him her biggest smile, and turns to face him.) "Sure, big fella, what took you so long to ask? Why sleep when I can love my man? You've made my day—and my night! Let's go!"

Is this how she reacts? I don't think so. She's disgusted. Not surprised, but disgusted.

> Woman: "What? Oh, come on! You can't be serious!
> What time is it? Are you crazy? Can't you
> control your hormones and wait?"

Whether this couple has sex or not, the wife feels used. She is not prepared in any way to be a cooperative, interested participant. She's nothing more than a filling station!

Sound familiar, ladies? I'll bet it does. If it's any consolation, your Caveman isn't the only husband groping in the middle of the night. Many wives have experienced the sexual thrill of the late-night, early-morning Casanova.

Of course, I—a highly trained Christian psychologist who conducts marriage seminars across the country—would never engage in such crude, selfish behavior. When I'm ready for sex, I notify Sandy three days in advance with a romantic card on her pillow. On the day of sex, I clean the entire home from top to bottom, help the kids with their homework, cook the evening meal, and then make sure the kids are confined to their rooms. I lead my queen into the boudoir, where she is greeted by soft music and rose petals scattered on the bed.

All right. That's enough. I'm making myself sick. The truth is, I don't always do a great job asking Sandy for sex. I have improved in preparing her for making love, but I have to admit I have been guilty of midnight and early-morning groping.

Sex is just one area where I—and the rest of the men reading this—have exhibited classic Caveman selfishness. The Caveman is usually not selfish in a mean-spirited, pathological way. He's not consciously and with evil intent trying to hurt his wife. His tendency to think of himself and his needs first is a genetic, automatic mechanism built into his Caveman brain.

Unfortunately, he does hurt his precious wife—over and over again—with his selfishness.

Caveman, it's time to stop the selfishness. I will begin my attack on the problem with some examples of selfishness from my own life.

The Miracle of the Grapefruit

I'm like many Cavemen. My mother unintentionally fostered my selfishness by spoiling me. From my birth through my high school years, she did my laundry. She cooked my meals and supplied me with my favorite snacks. She carted me to all my sports and other activities. She nursed me when I was sick.

So my selfishness is my mom's fault. No, not really. But her caring behavior did play a part in programming my already selfish male brain to think of myself first and expect a woman to meet my needs. Here's an example of Mom's influence.

Early in our marriage, Sandy and I were enjoying grapefruit one morning for breakfast. We were each eating half of a grapefruit, using spoons to scoop out the little sections.

I said, "Sandy, isn't it neat how the grapefruit has these little spoon-sized sections you can just scoop out? It's so convenient and easy. I guess it's one of God's little miracles."

Sandy looked at me strangely and said, "What are you talking about?" I replied, quite innocently, "You know, the grapefruit has these small, ready-to-eat separate sections."

Sandy laughed out loud, nearly choking on a grapefruit wedge. "Dave, the grapefruit doesn't come off the tree sectioned. Someone has to use a knife and section it by hand. I sectioned your half 20 minutes ago, before you came to the table."

Boy, did I feel dumb. You see, my mom had always sectioned my grapefruit for me. I took that for granted, never seeing the work that caused it to happen. My meals appeared on the table. My laundry appeared in my bureau drawers. My chauffeur took me where I wanted to go. I took it all for granted. I got used to having all these jobs done for me. Why, I deserved this kind of service, and my mom seemed happy to do it.

Always Leave a Little Behind

Here's a clever and incredibly selfish strategy I have followed for years: Never completely empty any container of food so you won't have to throw it out, clean the container, replace the food item, or be accused of eating food someone else wanted.

I never finish a box of cereal. I leave a handful of crumbs and shavings so someone else is forced to finish it, throw out the box, and put *cereal* on the grocery list. Brilliant, isn't it? I walk away free and clear! I follow the same strategy for milk, chips, cookies, any food in a bag, and leftovers. Believe me, leaving three green beans on a plate in the refrigerator takes guts.

I've been known to leave one or two squares of toilet paper on the roll so I don't have to replace it. Sick, isn't it?

I'm Sick! Help Me!

Speaking of being sick, that's when I'm really at my selfish best. For me, being struck by an illness, even if it's just the sniffles, is a major event. I act as though I've contracted smallpox and am barely hanging on to life. I want the whole world to stop for me. I want sympathy. I want attention. I want to be served. I don't want anyone to expect me to do any chores during my recovery. I want Sandy to kindly and lovingly nurse me back to health. Is that so wrong?

Yes, it is wrong. And selfish. Of course, when Sandy gets sick, she's on her own. I expect her to suck it up and carry on.

Birth-Control Nightmare

Another shocking example of Dave Clarke's selfishness occurred in 1994. Sandy was pregnant with our fourth child, William. It was a bit of a surprise. Okay, it was shocking. But we recovered nicely and began discussing the pros and cons of having a fifth child. After about ten seconds, we decided that four would be enough. Something had to be done, and quickly, or we'd end up with 17 kids. All I had to do was look at Sandy, and she became pregnant.

I naturally assumed that Sandy would just get her tubes tied after delivering William. I mean, wouldn't that be the easiest solution? Most of our friends had done that and seemed perfectly happy about it. Besides, how could a man who falls apart when he gets a cold possibly survive an operation where a very sharp object is used to cut his private parts? And this happens while he's fully conscious! It's barbaric! It's wrong! It's not fair! It's terribly painful! It's too expensive! (I wonder how many men have died from vasectomies.)

I was thinking all this, but fortunately I didn't say any of it to Sandy. I'll never forget the brief conversation we had when we decided on a permanent birth-control solution:

Sandy: "You're thinking I'm going to get my tubes tied, aren't you?"

Dave: (Being a moderately intelligent man, I said nothing.)

Sandy: "I've been through three pregnancies. I carried each child for nine months. I endured the extreme pain of three deliveries, pain you would never even remotely understand. I dealt with all the aches and pains and changes in my body. And now I'm pregnant for the fourth time and will do it all over again. I ask you, Dave, what do you think we should do to prevent all this from happening a fifth time?"

Dave: (In times of crisis and confusion, and when Sandy has that certain look on her face, I've always found it helpful to go with this question): "What do you think, dear?"

Sandy: "You'll get a vasectomy two weeks from today. Here's your appointment card. Good luck!"

Dave: "Yes, ma'am. That was just the solution I was considering. Thank you for setting it up so quickly."

Even though I knew the vasectomy procedure was a piece of cake and nothing like vaginal delivery pain, I still had to milk it for all it was worth. I mean, I did go under the knife for my woman. I suffered pain for her. I was her birth-control hero. Actually, Sandy did appreciate my effort and allowed me to get a little mileage out of my two-day recuperation. It only hurt for a few hours, but she didn't have to know that.

A Caveman's Just Gotta Have Fun!

Looking back over the years of my marriage, I've been undeniably selfish in the area of entertainment. I have controlled the television remote. I have watched too many hours of sports on television. I have chosen to play golf and go to sporting events with the guys when that time would have been better spent with Sandy and the kids.

Cavemen like to have fun, and they tend to spend too much time indulging themselves in their hobbies: surfing the net, playing video games, watching sports on television, playing softball, shooting hoops, golfing, bowling, hunting, fishing, skiing, working out at the gym, reading the paper...

You'd think there would be no real defense of selfishness. Oh, but there is. Here are some common Caveman justifications for selfish behavior, followed by my responses:

The Dialogue	
Caveman:	"I work hard for a living."
Me:	"Who doesn't? Your wife is working just as hard as you are, and she needs your help. Besides, the Bible says your most important job is meeting the needs of your wife."
Caveman:	"I'm doing my share around the home. I carry my weight around there."
Me:	"What you think really doesn't matter. What matters is what your dear wife thinks. She's the one you need to please. When she says you're doing your share, you're doing your share."
Caveman:	"I do more than my dad did and more than a lot of guys I know."

Me: "Your wife isn't married to your dad or these other guys, is she? Comparing yourself to other husbands is just a way to avoid facing the reality that you're not meeting your wife's needs."

Caveman: "I don't hang out in bars, drink like a fish, use drugs, or chase women."

Me: "Yeah, well, I hope not. I'll bet you're not a serial killer either. You want credit for that? Your wife has higher expectations for you."

Caveman: "I can never please her. Nothing is ever good enough for her."

Me: "Well, we won't know until you try, will we? You're probably doing things *you* think she needs, and you're probably wrong. Put together two months of solid effort meeting her actual needs, and then we'll see if she's pleased."

Caveman: "She's not thankful for what she has. Lots of women would love to have the life she has."

Me: "I'm not sure there would be a line out the door. I know living with you is a tremendous privilege, but that isn't the point. The point is, are you meeting her needs on a regular basis?"

Why So Selfish?

There are five central reasons for the selfish streak in men. One, it's a guy thing. We're born this way. Two, our dads probably modeled selfish behavior. Three, our moms probably modeled acceptance and enablement of our dad's selfishness. Four, our moms catered too much to our needs and spoiled us. Five, our wives feed our selfishness by being too caring and nurturing.

Whatever the reasons, now is the time for change. When we focus too much on *our* needs, we fail to notice and meet our wives' needs.

And that's wrong. Our selfishness hurts our wives and causes us to violate God's Ephesians 5:25 command: "Husbands, love your wives, just as Christ also loved the church and gave Himself up for her."

Christ sacrificed everything, including His life, for the church. Husbands are to sacrifice everything, including our selfish interests, for our wives. Their needs are more important than our needs.

Being selfish for the first part of your marriage is not a crime. Staying selfish *is* a crime. I have worked hard, and am still working hard, to change my selfish behavior and meet Sandy's needs. Now it's your turn.

Assume Nothing

The Caveman will often assume that his wife is happy and satisfied if no obvious problems or disturbances are interrupting his comfortable lifestyle. He thinks to himself, *Hey, if she's cooking meals, doing the chores, taking care of the kids, and having sex with me, things must be okay.*

The Caveman, in his selfish way, will make this assumption: *If I'm happy, she's happy.* Not necessarily.

The light may begin to dawn if the woman holds a gun to his head and says, "It's all over, slimeball. I'm taking you out." At this point, the Caveman will realize a problem exists. *Oh, I think she's a little unhappy with our relationship.*

Caveman, do not assume your woman is happy and feeling loved. She could be dying inside. The fact that she continues to do the chores, cook, and have sex does not mean you are meeting her needs.

The typical Caveman truly believes he knows what his wife's needs are, and he's confident he's doing a terrific job meeting them. He's shocked to find out in my therapy office that he has no clue what her needs are and that he's not even close to meeting them.

I say the same thing to all the Cavemen I see in therapy: "Your wife defines whether or not you meet her needs, not you! If she says you're not meeting her needs, you're not meeting her needs. The only way to know her needs is to ask her...frequently."

Ask Her What Her Needs Are

Stop assuming you know her needs and ask her. Not asking is like throwing darts in a pitch-dark room. You have no idea where the dartboard is! You must ask her often because she'll change her mind. She is an emotional, moody, and unpredictable creature.

Ask her in the morning, before you go your separate ways. "Honey, what are your needs today? What can I do for you today?" We hope she'll be telling you what her needs are, but you ask anyway. When you ask, have a writing pad handy and jot down her needs. You use lists for your job, don't you?

You can choose to not write down her needs. Then you are sure to forget. She'll be upset that you forgot. She'll be upset that you didn't meet her needs. You'll be upset because she's upset. You'll have to spend the evening listening to her vent, saying you're sorry 45 times, and trying to reassure her that you do love her. Or you can write down her needs and spend a pleasant evening with a warm, loving woman whose needs have been met by her loving husband.

Ask her at lunchtime or in the early afternoon by phone. "Sweetheart, have your needs changed since this morning? Can I do anything else for you today?" Again, write down any changes or additions on your pad. She'll love the fact that you called because it reveals that you're thinking about her. And you'll catch any new needs she may have.

Ask her in the evening as soon as you see her. "Sweetie, I love you. What can I do for you tonight?" Jot down her needs and spend the first part of the evening taking care of them. With any luck, one of her requests may be, "Make wild love to me after the kids are in bed." If you're asking for and meeting her needs on a daily basis, this kind of request won't be out of the question.

Ask her just before bed. "Honey, do you know what your needs will be tomorrow?" Jot down what she says on your pad. That's a nice, loving way to end the day.

Caveman, I know what you're thinking. *You're kidding, right? No husband I know asks for his wife's needs four times a day and writes them on a pad.* No, I'm not kidding. True, very few husbands do what I am suggesting. Those who don't are the ones with unhappy, resentful, and cold wives. Those who do are the ones with happy, satisfied, and warm wives. Those who do are following the example of Jesus: "The Son of Man did not come to be served, but to serve" (Matthew 20:28).

If You Can't Meet One of Her Needs, Tell Her Why

Your wife suffers when she thinks you ignore her and don't explain why you don't meet her needs. It's a double whammy. Her needs go unmet—that's one whammy. She has no explanation of why they went unmet—that's the other whammy.

The woman wants to know why. Not knowing why bothers her. If it bothers her, sooner or later it will bother you, Caveman. She may not mean to make you pay for your lack of information, but you will pay.

Caveman, when your woman asks you to meet a need or when you ask her what she needs, train yourself to respond as soon as possible in one of two ways.

Yes, with a Plan and Timetable

Write down—immediately—her need and your plan for meeting it. Make sure your wife agrees with your plan. This procedure is not just to provide your wife with peace of mind and security. It ensures you won't blow it and fail to meet her need.

> "I'll call the plumber before noon today and schedule him to come to the house tomorrow between three and four."
>
> "I'll mow the lawn and edge by Saturday at six."
>
> "I'll vacuum the living room by the end of the evening."

Remember, when you say you'll do something for your woman, you've made a promise. If you don't do it the way you said you'd do it or when you said you'd do it, she'll feel betrayed. Trust is damaged. She'll feel unloved and unimportant. You'll have to spend time doing damage control.

No, with an Explanation

Your wife needs to know why the answer is no. Don't leave her hanging. Tell her right up front your reason for not meeting one of her needs. If you say yes but later realize you won't be able to meet a need, tell her as soon as possible the reason you can't do it.

"I'm tired."

"I don't have the time today."

"I'm angry at you."

"I have something else I have to do."

"I have an unexpected meeting at work."

"I didn't realize the store closed at five."

You may well have a legitimate reason to say no. You are far better off saying no with an explanation than saying yes and not coming through. No with an explanation gives her closure, and she can drop it. A woman without closure is not a pretty sight! She'll keep picking at you or stay hurt inside about it.

Get Regular Feedback

Caveman, ask your wife on a regular basis how effectively you're meeting her needs. You have to get feedback to do a good job. When you're learning this new system, ask her every day how you're doing. "Am I meeting your needs, honey? How can I improve?"

Even after you've gotten the hang of it, ask her for feedback every few days. At a minimum, ask her once a week for an evaluation. This keeps you on track and is a great way to express love for her. Act on her feedback.

Marriage Enrichment Steps

1. Can you admit that you tend to be selfish? Tell your wife some recent examples of your selfishness.

2. Ask your wife to share a recent example of your selfish behavior.

3. What are your reasons or excuses for acting in selfish ways? Which excuses from the Dialogue section (pages 50-51) have you used?

4. Where does your selfish behavior come from? Did you learn it growing up in your home? What kind of selfish behavior did your dad model for you? Did your mom cater to you? Has your wife enabled your selfish behavior?

5. How do you think you're doing meeting your wife's needs? After you give your assessment, ask your wife how she thinks you're doing.

6. Are you willing to follow the strategy I describe at the end of the chapter? Right now, ask your wife for a list of needs for tomorrow and jot them down on your pad. Agree to meet tomorrow evening to talk about how effectively you met those needs.

5

Cinderella, You're Trying Too Hard

Classic Female Communication Mistakes

The communication problems between Cavemen and Cinderellas go all the way back to birth. Our God-ordained differences are wonderful, but they get in the way of connecting on a deep level in conversation.

Most Cavemen are naturally doers, not talkers, and they have a built-in drive to avoid emotional intimacy. Most Cinderellas are born talkers and have a built-in craving for emotional intimacy.

A Disaster Waiting to Happen

Boys and girls grow up, but their basic differences in communication styles don't change.

The Caveman is action oriented and conversationally challenged. He will talk, but only on a superficial level. He naturally shies away from emotional connection. He wants to *do* things with you, like watch the ball game or do a physical activity or share a hobby or have sex. A lot of sex. He is satisfied with a fairly shallow level of emotional intimacy.

Cinderella is talk oriented and conversationally focused. She wants to talk on a deeper level rather than on just an intellectual or informational level. She has an intense desire to emotionally connect. She doesn't mind doing things with you as long as you'll talk with her and create an emotional bond. She is very disappointed and hurt by the lack of emotional intimacy in your marriage. She can't be truly happy without it.

Great combination, huh? Actually, it's a disaster waiting to happen. And it does happen. Driven by these differences, the Caveman and Cinderella each make critical mistakes in the area of communication and emotional intimacy.

Because of the critical importance of communication in marriage, I'm devoting the next four chapters to it. This chapter and the next will be for Cinderella: one on her mistakes in communication and one giving her the tools to talk to and connect with her husband. The following two chapters will be for the Caveman: one on his mistakes in communication, and one helping him talk to and connect with his wife.

Cinderella, brace yourself. You're going first.

Women Are Born Talkers

Sandy and I have a son and three beautiful daughters. The girls love to talk. They live to talk. There aren't enough hours in the day to handle all their words. Leeann and Nancy even talk in their sleep.

My girls talk with us and with each other. They talk on the phone with their friends. They "talk" on the computer in long, expressive e-mails and in instant messages. I haven't spoken on the phone or used my computer at home for two years. I can't get on either one. The girls' supply of conversational information is endless. My Emily will spend three hours with some friends at a party, talking all the time. When she gets home, she'll go immediately to the computer so she can talk with these same friends about what they just talked about.

My girls jump from topic to topic, and every topic, no matter how trivial, is important because it can lead to a whole chain of interesting conversational tidbits. Here's a recent conversation (actually, a monologue) I had with my daughter Leeann:

> Dad, that's a nice shirt you are wearing. Is that a light green stripe? My friend Bobbi was wearing a skirt two weeks ago

with a light green stripe. She got into trouble with her mom because her skirt was too short. They had a bad argument out by their pool. The pool was dirty, so her mom blamed her for that too. Her little dog, Fluffy, a white and brown wiener dog who has kidney problems, came running up just then and tried to jump into her arms. Bobbi didn't see her coming, so she jerked back in surprise, and Fluffy jumped right into the pool. It was hilarious! You know, I saw another dog last Thursday that looked like Fluffy. By the way, did I mention that I saw Fluffy once? Bobbi brought her to school one morning. That was the same morning that I broke my favorite yellow hairbrush. I loved that hairbrush. Anyway, this other dog was wearing a cute little red and black checkered vest. My friend Ashley had bought that same kind of vest last March when we were shopping at the mall. Can you believe that? I remember the salesperson had bright purple hair, a nose ring, and a bad attitude. She was rude to Ashley and me. Oh, there were so many weird things that happened that day at the mall! We were just getting dropped off at the entrance by her mom when…

This was the first two and half minutes of the conversation! Leeann was just getting warmed up. I don't have room to list the topics Leeann covered in the other 20 minutes. You see how important noticing the green stripe was? Women talk the way paleontologists create prehistoric animal models for museums. From one chipped tooth, these scientists build an entire dinosaur. Women can easily build an entire conversation from one, tiny, inconsequential fact. Amazing!

Raised to Create Closeness

Your typical woman isn't just *born* to create closeness. She's also *raised* to create it. Her mom, her grandmothers, her aunts, her sisters, her schoolteachers, and other significant women in her life gave her thousands and thousands of lessons in the fine art of communication. These ladies not only modeled how to talk and emotionally connect, they practiced connecting with her over and over again. She was in a daily seminar from birth until she married, and she earned a doctorate in conversational intimacy.

Two women having a conversation create an incredible sight to behold. They fill the air with words, talk at the same time, laugh at the same time, and don't even seem to take a breath. They effortlessly reflect back to each other the content and emotions of the conversation. They give empathy and compassion without even thinking about it. They connect.

How the Wife Kills Intimacy

While the Caveman is busy avoiding intimacy (more on this in chapter 7), Cinderella is hard at work accidentally killing intimacy. She's geared to go after closeness in relationships, so she tends to be too intense with her husband. She tries too hard to get close, and when she can't get connected, her powerful reaction drives the man further away.

Cinderella's mistakes prevent the deeper communication and emotional intimacy she so desperately wants. She turns her Caveman away from conversation, from romance, and from treating her the way she wants to be treated.

Here are some common ways a wife kills intimacy.

The Nagging Witch

You are way too aggressive in your attempts to get your husband to open up and talk personally. In your drive to get some intimacy with your man, you are too direct and apply too much pressure. You pepper him with questions. You press him for responses. You want him to tell you what he thinks and how he feels, and you want him to do it now. You bring up the same topic over and over, hoping that he'll finally talk about it. You follow him down the hall.

You are a nagging witch, and without realizing it, you are killing conversations and robbing yourself of the intimacy you long for. Your actions are more like involuntary manslaughter because you do not intend to do this. You continually back your Caveman into conversational corners. He feels threatened and controlled, so he will not give you the dialogue you want. He'll clam up and say nothing, snap at you in anger and frustration, or leave the room. Sound familiar?

Your style of trying to force your husband to talk turns the attempt into a complete failure. You succeed only in shutting him up and driving him further away from you. He thinks you're attacking his manhood and independence. And guess what—he's right. Your intensity becomes the only issue in his mind. As he fends off your high-pressure approach, all he's thinking is, *What a nag! What's her problem? I wish she'd back off! I just want to get away from this screaming meemie!*

She Who Is Always Right

When you get emotional and upset, you have a tendency to think you're right. You feel very strongly about the issue, and your emotional intensity can carry you to a place where you feel moral and intellectual superiority. You forget that you're engrossed by *your* opinion and *your* feelings.

You often don't want to hear your Caveman's opinion unless he agrees with you. If he disagrees, you get even more agitated and launch into a combination of lecture and finger-pointing.

I can't tell you how many men—actually, its 52,134—who have told me privately, "Dave, I'm always wrong! Whenever she gets angry or hurt, no matter what has happened, I'm wrong. She doesn't want to hear my point of view." (This is strange because the wives are desperate to know how their husbands feel.)

This bumper sticker says it all: If a man was talking in a forest and no woman was there to hear him, would he still be wrong?

The Woman Who Talks Too Much

There's just no delicate way to say it. You talk too much. You fill the air with words, tossing topic after topic at your poor Caveman. You don't pause. You just keep going. You think that conversation with your husband is like throwing spaghetti against the wall. Sooner or later, something has to stick. I mean, one of your topics has to arouse his interest. He has to respond to something you say!

No, actually he doesn't. And he won't. He simply can't process all the sentences and paragraphs gushing from your mouth. Your waves of words overwhelm his tiny brain, and it will explode. He shuts down. He gets distracted. He tunes you out. He goes into a different zone, staring into the distance with no expression on his face. You notice you've lost him, you get upset, and the conversation is over. Actually, a conversation never happened in the first place. It was just you talking.

During those infrequent times when he does speak, you don't let him finish. You interrupt him. You ask too many questions. You ask for more details. You want him to clarify statements. You make too many observations. You cut in and ask him to share his emotional reaction to the events he's describing: "But honey, how did that make you *feel?*"

You're driving him crazy, and most importantly, you're choking off any possibility he'll keep talking and maybe go a little deeper. Your interruptions make him lose his train of thought. He can only focus on one topic at a time. He simply cannot follow all the different ideas, interruptions, and rabbit trails you're throwing at him.

You think you're giving him multiple opportunities to respond. In reality, you are burying him alive with your torrent of words. His brain circuits are overloaded, he gets frustrated, and he stops talking.

Talk to Me—Right Now!

Cinderella, you have a bad habit of expecting your Caveman to respond immediately to your conversational offerings. You want to know what he's thinking and feeling about what you're talking about, and you want to know *right now*. The truth is that your Caveman cannot give you a personal response that quickly.

You're convinced he knows what he's thinking and feeling about the topic and is simply keeping it to himself. The nerve! The utter gall of the man! Why would he be holding out on you? I'll tell you why.

Because he has no idea what he's thinking and feeling. At least not yet. He needs time to consider what you're saying and develop his personal reaction.

First, his brain moves a lot slower than yours in the area of deeper, more personal sharing. Second, he is not in constant contact with his emotions (as you are), so he needs to dig down and find them. Third, unlike you, he does not discover his emotions as he talks out loud in conversation. For him, locating emotions is a very private, internal matter.

The bottom line is this: Your Caveman needs time and space to process what you're saying so he can figure out his personal reaction to it.

When you ask him to tell you about his emotions, which you have every right to do, he literally can't answer right then. He has no clue how he's feeling yet. He'll have a delayed reaction to just about every request for his emotions. He may be able to find some feelings about the topic 30 minutes later, a few hours later, or a few days later. If you press him to identify his emotions on the spot, he'll shut down and stop talking. And that will be your fault, not his.

Your Timing Is Terrible

I know you and your Caveman can never seem to find a good time to have a deeper, more personal talk. He is famous for coming up with all kinds of excuses for why "this isn't a good time to talk." Believe me, I'm aware of all the Caveman tricks to weasel out of conversation. I've used them all myself. But you should be aware of some very bad times to try to engage your Caveman in a deeper type of conversation.

Don't try to talk with him when he's hungry. His need for food is all he can think about: *Starving. Getting weaker. Must...have...suste-nance...or...can't...go...on.* I know this is pathetic, but that's the way it is. A Caveman has enough trouble talking on a full stomach. If his stomach is empty, he doesn't have a chance.

Don't try to talk with him when he's tired. Talking with you requires a great deal of energy, and when he is physically and mentally fatigued, he simply doesn't have the capacity to do it. He's not asleep yet, but his brain waves are pretty slow. His system is gradually shutting down. He can watch television, feed his face with a snack, and give one- or two-word answers to simple questions. But he certainly cannot engage in a personal, meaningful conversation. You need to catch him before this shut-down process begins in the evening.

Don't try to talk to your Caveman when he's in bed. He may be too tired to talk (see above paragraph). Or, even worse, he'll be in an amorous mood and move into groping mode: *Woman...in...nightgown...been...a...couple...of...days...must...have...sex.* For a Caveman, the bed is for sleeping or for sex. Not for talking.

Don't try to talk with him when he's just arrived home from work. He is stressed, preoccupied, and trying to make the transition from work to home. He needs at least 30 minutes to change clothes, relax a little, and unwind from the day's headaches.

Don't try to talk with him when he's doing any other activity: watching television, reading the paper, using the computer, searching for food in the fridge...Your basic Caveman can only do one thing at a time. He is easily distracted. Talking with you will require his total attention and concentration.

The Dialogue

Cinderella: "What do you mean, I talk too much?"

Me: "It's not that you talk too much. It's that you talk too much for your Caveman. Another woman could listen to you for hours. His attention span isn't that long. Twenty to thirty minutes at a sitting is his limit."

Cinderella: "My husband says I ask him too many questions."

Me: "He's right. You're the queen of interrogation. You're overwhelming him. You press for too much information too soon. 'What about this? What about that? How do you feel? What are you thinking about right now?' Stop pumping him! He feels as if he's being given the third degree with a bright light in his face. You're going to have to limit your questions."

Cinderella: "The one thing I want and need more than anything else is for him to tell me what he's thinking and feeling. You know, personal stuff. He knows I need this kind of sharing, but he refuses to do it. He deliberately clams up even though he sees how it hurts me."

Me: "He doesn't open up and share because he feels pressured and because he doesn't know what he's thinking and feeling. If you keep pressing him, he'll clam up even tighter. You need to back off and let him find out what's inside."

Cinderella: "Okay, let me see if I understand this. I can't talk too much. I can't ask too many questions. I can't think I'm right just because I'm emotional about an issue. I can't pressure him to share his feelings and thoughts immediately. And I can't try to have a deep conversation with him when he's hungry, tired, in bed, just home from work, or doing any other activity which would distract him. So how am I supposed to talk with this man and get the closeness I need?"

Me: "I'm glad you asked. You have a good handle on what not to do. Now you need to know what you can do. I've developed some successful strategies that will help you build better and deeper conversations with your Caveman."

Great Conversations Are Within Your Reach

Sandy will admit that she made these five communication mistakes. She didn't intentionally kill our intimacy, but it died all the same. Of course, I was busy killing our intimacy with my own unintentional mistakes.

We worked hard to identify our mistakes, and we fixed them. So can you and your husband.

I've explained your mistakes in communication. Now I'll tell you how to connect with your Caveman in conversation.

Marriage Enrichment Steps

1. Wife, tell your husband about your childhood. How much of a talker were you? Who were the women who taught you how to talk, express your feelings, and create closeness? How did they teach you?

2. Wife, describe your mom—her personality, the time she spent with you, and how she communicated her feelings. What kind of marriage did your mom and dad have as you grew up? How did they communicate, resolve conflicts, and show affection? Did you think your mom was disappointed with her marriage in any way? How are you like your mom?

3. Wife, answer question 2 again, but this time, apply it to your dad.

4. Wife, tell your husband which of the five intimacy-killing mistakes you believe you have used most often. Ask him which ones he feels you are guilty of the most. Ask him to lovingly catch you using these turn-offs so you can stop doing them.

6

Cinderella,
Back Off

Talk Less, Talk Smart, and Let Him Pursue

One of the most common questions I hear from wives is this: "Dave, what can I do to get my husband to open up and talk personally with me?" The heart's desire of nearly every woman is to regularly connect on a deeper level in conversation with her husband. That's why she married him. That's what she wants and needs more than anything else.

I always give the same two answers to this question. "First, you've got to stop making Cinderella mistakes in communication." (I described these mistakes in the last chapter.) "Second, you must learn some effective communication tools if you want your husband to open up and share his personal, inside information with you."

Here are the communication strategies that will help you develop deeper, more meaningful conversations with your Caveman.

Thirty-Minute Daily Talk Times

Regularly scheduled talk times create opportunities for deeper conversations with your Caveman. These 30-minute talk times (at least four days a week) are critical and foundational prerequisites for conversational intimacy. If a couple is going to connect in communication, they need specific, intentional, no-distractions-allowed, focused times together.

I recommend the two of you have as many daily talk times as possible. One a day is the ultimate goal. Five or even six a week would be great. My counseling experience has shown that you will need at least four to develop deeper talks.

I believe the husband, as the leader, is responsible to make sure these talk times happen each week. However, usually the wife must be the first to bring up this strategy. Perhaps a bit down the road, the husband will step up and take the lead in this area.

Cinderella, sit down with your husband when the kids aren't around and you aren't distracted, and present your case with words like these:

> Honey, it's very important to me that we spend regular time together in conversation. I think it's also very important for us and our relationship. Our usual hit-or-miss, "talk when we get a chance" style is keeping us from the kind of closeness I think we need. I don't want to settle for an okay marriage. I want a great marriage, and talking more during the week will help us get there.
>
> I'd like to have a 30-minute talk time every day of the week. This may be a little unrealistic, so let's shoot for seven days but get at least four or five. Every Saturday or Sunday, let's sit down and schedule our talk times for the upcoming week. We'll select the four or five days that look the best for us. We'll put these appointments on the calendar, in our Day-Timers, and in our PDAs.
>
> We need to enjoy our talk times in a quiet, comfortable, and private place at home. We can't allow any distractions. No television, no kids, no pets, no phones, no magazines or newspapers, and no computer. Just the two of us alone.
>
> These four or five talk times will help me stop nagging and pressuring you to talk. I won't have to talk your head off, as I do now during those few times during the week when I try to get your attention. I'll be able to relax and save most of my talking for these specific times. We'll be closer, and I'll be happier. I really think this will make me more interested in sex and more responsive in bed [this will definitely get his attention].

Post a Talk-Time Schedule

> Once we have selected the days we will have a talk time, I'd like us to post a talk-time schedule for that week. Let's say we choose Monday, Wednesday, Thursday, and Friday. We write these days on a piece of paper with a column under each day. If we have a topic we'd like to discuss on a certain day, we jot it down in the column under that day. For example, if I want to talk about the pastor's sermon during our Monday talk time, I'd jot that topic under the Monday column.

> This system will not only help us remember what we want to talk about but also be a good way to continue talking about certain topics. For example, if either one of us wants to continue talking about the pastor's sermon after Monday, we can write that topic in the Wednesday column. If one of us wants to talk about the sermon again, we can write it in the Thursday column.

> Let's post this talk-time schedule someplace where we'll both see it every day, like the refrigerator, the kitchen door, or the big mirror in our bedroom.

After asking him for his response and getting his input on the regular talk times and the posted schedule, ask him to pray with you about it. After the prayer, ask him to think and pray about these ideas for two or three days. Set a day and time to come back together to discuss these strategies and make some decisions.

At this second meeting, assuming he is willing to try these strategies, the two of you will schedule your first four talk times and post your talk-time schedule.

These foundational communication strategies will create real intimacy by allowing you to apply the carryover principle. To achieve depth in conversation, Cinderella and the Caveman must talk about the same topic two, three, or even four times. Each time you talk about the topic, you get a little deeper.

The Caveman cannot express his personal thoughts and feelings about a topic in the first conversation about it. He needs time to process and figure out what's inside. With this system, he can process and revisit the topic in the next two or three scheduled talk times. Rather than dying an early and untimely death, a topic can live on into the next few talk times.

It's Time to Talk Smart

Cinderella, you consistently make two major mistakes when you're talking with your Caveman. (I have already discussed these mistakes, but they are so important I must repeat them.) First, you use too many words and overwhelm his limited listening apparatus. He has attention deficit disorder when you talk too much. He just can't take it!

When you rattle on for too long, which means anything over five minutes, even a Caveman with decent listening skills can't hang in there with you. As you drone on, here's what he's thinking:

> *What was point number eight?*
>
> *I'm drowning in her ocean of details!*
>
> *Please, get to the main point!*
>
> *I'm begging you, move on!*
>
> *Stop beating a dead horse!*
>
> *Stop the torture! I give up! I'll tell you where the important papers are!*
>
> *Lord, please come now and rescue me from this agony.*

Your Caveman will lose his concentration. He won't be able to focus. He'll get overloaded. He'll tune you out. When he tunes you out, you'll catch him as you always do, and the conversation is over. You're angry and hurt, he's a dirtball who doesn't care about you, and life stinks.

Your second mistake is expecting your Caveman to be able to respond immediately to what you're saying. You want his personal thoughts, emotions, and reactions, and you want them right now. You fail to realize that your Caveman has a very slow processor, and he needs time—from two hours to two days or more—to study what you've said and figure out a personal response.

Cinderella, these two mistakes are killing the majority of your conversations with your Caveman. You need to talk smart with your Caveman, and I have a strategy that will help you do that. I call it one-way communication.

One-Way Communication

In one-way communication, you *briefly* tell your Caveman your view, your thoughts, and your emotions about a topic and *do not expect an immediate reply*. I call it one-way because you do all the talking.

You tell him he doesn't have to respond. You ask him to listen and concentrate in order to understand, to take time to process what you've said, and then, when he's ready, to share his reaction. When you're done talking, you either walk away or simply go silent. If you're with him at home in a couple talk time, in the car, in a restaurant, or out somewhere, just be quiet for at least five minutes. You can continue in silence or bring up another topic of conversation.

You speak your piece and move on. Unlike what you've done in the past, you do not press him for an immediate reaction. Why not? Two reasons. First, men cannot respond right away. They need time to process and figure out their feelings and thoughts on an issue. Personal issues require even more time. Second, men will always clam up when they feel pressured by women. They feel controlled, and they demonstrate with their silence that no one can make them talk.

If you express yourself *in five minutes or less* and allow him time to process, you increase the likelihood that your man will consider what you say and get back to you to continue the conversation. If you nag him or even ask him sweetly for a quick response, your man will harden up and never respond on that topic. Never. My way, the one-way communication strategy, gets you a maybe. Your way, the natural Cinderella way of pushing him to say something back right away, gets you a never. Try it my way.

You can try several different types of one-way communication. Let's take a look at them.

The Five-Minute Burst During Couple Talk Time

For regular, no-conflict couple talk times, try the five-minute one-way burst. As you begin speaking, ask him right up front to listen and reflect back to you what he hears. As you talk, check in with him periodically to make sure he's engaged with you: "Are you with me, honey?" "Do you understand what I'm saying?" "What emotion do you think I'm feeling right now?" You're not asking for his response to what you're saying. You're seeing if he understands the basic content and your emotions.

Talk for five minutes and then stop. Give him a chance to think, to digest what you've said, and to prepare some kind of a response. He might say something back, or he might not. At least by pausing you've given him an opportunity to connect with you.

If he says nothing during your pause, let five minutes go by. Don't jump right back in with more comments on the same topic. Talk about another topic for five minutes, and pause again. If he doesn't respond, let ten minutes go by. By being silent more often, you might motivate him to initiate more conversations. He'll notice your silence and may talk more to draw you back closer to him.

At the end of your 30-minute talk time, tell him the one or two topics you'd like him to process and get back to you on. Tell him you'll jot these topics on the talk-time schedule under the day of your next meeting. Or tell him he can do it. This is the best way to remind him you want to hear what he has to say on these topics.

The Five-Minute Burst at Other Times

Obviously, you and your Caveman will talk outside of the four or five couple talk times each week. In these times, make sure you have his full attention. Then, talk for five minutes or fewer about a topic. Tell him you'd like him to think about what you've said and to get back to you with his response when he's ready. Tell him he can respond before your next scheduled talk time (you should be so lucky!), or he can wait until the talk time. Go ahead and jot the topic on the talk-time schedule under the day of your next meeting. If he happens to respond before the meeting (miracles do happen!), you can just cross that item off the talk-time schedule.

The 30-Second Burst When He Fails to Respond

What if you speak one-way and he still doesn't come back to you with a response? Well, he is a Caveman, and that's certainly going to happen a lot. When you've waited a day or two and he clearly has no intention of giving you a response, take two steps.

Step one is to give him one low-key, no-emotion reminder. You get only one. If you remind him twice, you're a nagging witch. In 30 seconds or fewer, say something like this: "Remember that issue we discussed? When you're ready, I'd like you to find me and give me your reaction to what I said." You could also add, "I'll put this topic on the talk-time schedule for our next meeting." After these statements, say nothing else about it. Move on.

If he still won't talk about it, go to step two. Go to him and give him a one-way communication that expresses your feelings about his decision to ignore you and refuse to respond to the topic. Say something like this: "I'm angry and disappointed that you've chosen to not come back to me about (whatever issue you had brought up). That makes me feel unloved and unimportant. I just wanted you to know." Then, drop it and walk away. Don't bring it up again.

This cleans your system of anger and resentment, allows you to forgive him, and gives you closure on the issue. And just maybe he will feel bad and come back to you with a response to the issue.

The 30-Second Burst When He Doesn't Want to Talk

He's obviously upset about something. You ask him a reasonable question: "What's wrong?" He says, "Nothing." Instead of yelling, "Liar!" give him a 30-second burst with words like these:

"Look, I know something's wrong. I know it's hard for you to talk about it, so I won't try to pry it out of you. I want to comfort and support you, but I can't if you don't tell me what's bothering you. When you want to share what it is, come to me. You can share it a little at a time over several days, and I'll just listen and reflect back to you what I'm hearing."

The 30-Second Burst in Response to His Caveman Shtick

Until now, your responses to his Caveman behaviors have been ineffective. When he's killed conversation after conversation with his standard maneuvers to avoid intimacy, you've cried. You've yelled. Lectured. Whispered. Begged. Pleaded. Reasoned. Threatened. Ignored. Nothing has worked. He's still not talking, and you're still a wife with no intimacy.

Time to try something new, something that has a much better chance of working. I want you to respond to his classic Caveman communication-killing shtick with brief, verbal surgical strikes. The choreographed one-way responses I've included below will rattle your Caveman and create some real changes in your relationship. Besides, these snappy comebacks will keep you sane and give you some fun. When you live with a Caveman, you need some entertainment.

> Caveman: (He's not listening to you. His eyes are glazed over. He's in the zone.)
>
> Cinderella: "Brain cramp, huh? I'm insulted and angry because you're not paying attention to me. If you don't want to listen to me, say so. Let me know when you're ready to listen." (Stop talking and make him come to you to restart the conversation.)
>
> Caveman: (He falls silent as you talk. He gives no responses at all.)
>
> Cinderella: "You're not saying anything. I can't tell if you're listening. If you don't want to talk about this, tell me. If you're okay with this topic, give me some responses so I know

you're with me. It's frustrating to talk and get no feedback, so I won't do it. I'll wait for you to tell me what's on your mind."

Caveman: (He's not completely shut down, but his mind is somewhere else. He's giving you one- and two-word answers.)

Cinderella: "You seem out of it tonight. You're not involved in this conversation. I won't keep trying to get you interested in me and what I'm saying. I'll get angry and so will you. Come to me when you're ready to talk. I'd like to know what you're thinking about tonight, but you'll have to decide to tell me."

Caveman: (He's just dropped one of his logical conversation-killer comments on you: "You shouldn't feel that way." "You're too intense." "You're overreacting." "Simmer down, and I'll show you the facts." "You're wrong and I can prove it." "Here's how to fix your problem.")

Cinderella: "Hold it right there. I don't need logic. I'm not going to listen to it now. If I did, I'd get furious. What I need now is for you to listen to me, reflect back to me what I'm saying, and help me feel understood. When you're ready to do that, let me know. Once I feel understood, I'll be happy to listen to your logic."

Caveman: (You've asked him, "How was your day?" and he replies, "Fine" or "Okay.")

Cinderella: "That one word really doesn't tell me too much. I need more information than that. Take some time and think about your day, and then find me and tell me what you come up with."

Caveman: "I don't know."

Cinderella:	"When you do know, come and find me and tell me. We can't build a conversation on, 'I don't know.'"
Caveman:	"I don't want to talk about it."
Cinderella:	"Okay. I respect that. Please listen to me talk about it for five minutes. Hear me out. You don't have to give me your view now. After you think about what I've said and you're ready to talk, find me. Or you can wait until our next couple talk time."
Caveman:	"This isn't a good time to talk about it."
Cinderella:	"What if I tell you 'this isn't a good time' the next time you want sex? What sex is to you, communication is for me. When you're ready to talk about this, find me and we'll schedule a meeting."

Is this approach a little edgy? Yes. Will it be unnerving to your Caveman? Yes. Will it make you a challenge for him? Yes. Will it shake him out of his no-personal-sharing comfort zone and motivate him to pursue you and talk more? Quite possibly.

When He Talks

When your Caveman talks, let him talk and don't interrupt him. Don't ask him a bunch of questions. Don't jump ahead and make comments about where you think he's headed in the story. Don't bring up topics his story triggers in your mind. Don't press him for his emotional reaction.

Okay, that's what you don't do. Here's what you do. Let him be logical during the first part of the conversation. He's a logical creature, so he'll start with the facts and events only. Your job is to listen and reflect. By *reflect*, I mean briefly say back to him the content (the facts and his thoughts) and the emotion (his feelings about what he is saying).

Be very low-key when you reflect his emotions. Wait until he's expressed at least a few paragraphs and then tell him how you think he's feeling: "I'll bet that made you feel…" Just mention a few emotions and don't ask him to confirm your guesses or comment further on his emotional state. This strategy will help him identify his emotions and give him a head start on his processing.

After reflecting what he's said and how you think he's feeling, you can ask him a few (two or three at most) questions. Ask him to take some time to process and get back to you with his responses. Tell him you'd like to continue the talk on his topic when he's ready. One of you can put the topic on the talk-time schedule.

Let Him Pursue You

Stop chasing him. Stop using a direct, in-your-face approach to get him to talk. Stop pressuring him to talk. Stop nagging him to talk. Stop pouting and whining, hoping he'll feel guilty and talk. Stop talking too much.

All these behaviors put you in pursuit of him. That is not God's design for you, so it will never work. He is the leader (Ephesians 5:22-24), who is to pursue you with the same kind of love Christ has for the church (Ephesians 5:25-26).

If you pursue him, he will feel cornered and controlled and defensive. As a result, his walls will go way up, and he won't talk.

The strategies in this chapter work because they jibe with the way a Caveman communicates. They also work on a deeper level because they consistently make him the pursuer and you the pursued.

If you can get him to pursue you, you will change your entire communication system. A Caveman will communicate more deeply and personally when he's in pursuit of his woman.

Marriage Enrichment Steps

1. How often do the two of you have specific, intentional, scheduled, 30-minute talk times each week? What has kept you from having talks like these?

2. Are you willing to follow the strategy of scheduling at least four couple talk times a week? Right now, schedule your first four.

3. How will posting your talk-time schedule improve the depth of your communication as a couple? Where will you post this schedule?

4. Cinderella, how do you feel about the one-way communication strategy? Caveman, how do you feel about it? Which type of one-way communication will be the hardest to do? Which type do you think will help your communication as a couple the most?

5. Caveman, tell your Cinderella what she can be doing when you're talking that will help you communicate more deeply and personally. What strategy could she follow that would help you the most?

6. Who is the communication pursuer in the relationship? If it's you, Cinderella, are you willing to give up that role? Caveman, are you willing to pursue her? How will you do that?

7

Caveman, You're Avoiding Intimacy

Classic Male Communication Mistakes

Cinderella has taken her medicine. We have exposed her mistakes in communication and discussed the solutions. But I've only told half the story—half the equation—about communication.

Caveman, as they used to say in biblical times, it's time to "gird up your loins." In other words, hunker down. Batten down the hatches. You're in for a rough ride. It's your turn in the hot seat.

You, Caveman, are also making communication mistakes, and these mistakes are limiting the intimacy in your marriage. You need to change, so let's get to it.

Men Are Born Doers

God created William, our son. And there was destruction. And there was yelling, running, climbing, wild laughter, and loud animal noises. And constant activity. Seven-year-old William, like almost all boys—and men—is a doer. From the moment he gets up at the crack of dawn (he's slept in an extra hour exactly twice in his first seven years) to the moment he finally goes to sleep at night, William is doing something. He plays video games and computer games, engages in every outdoor sport known to man with his neighborhood buddies, rides his bike, swims in the pool, plays board games and card games, and bugs his sisters. If he watches television or a movie, it had better be sports oriented or filled with nonstop, dramatic action.

William does talk, but only about four things: what he's done, what he's doing right now, what he's going to do, and sports. If he's not doing something, he's miserable. He can't stand just sitting around and talking. He hates chick movies. He's not sensitive. His sisters' feelings aren't even on his radar. He just wants to play, play, play and do, do, do.

William, like most men, is a doer because he has a God-given need to compete with others and maintain control in relationships. If William is going to be a good husband someday, he will have to learn to open up and communicate with a woman. Sandy and I are trying to teach him these skills, but we face an uphill battle. It's against his nature, and he just doesn't get it...yet.

William has no desire to get in touch with his feelings. Even if, by some miracle, he did identify his feelings, he'd rather take a beating than express them to another person. Especially to a girl. He doesn't cry very often. That's for wimps and mamas' boys. He feels close to someone when they do something together.

Raised to Avoid Closeness

Your typical man isn't just born to avoid intimacy. He is also raised to avoid it. Watching his parents and their relationship taught him all he needed to know about sidestepping closeness.

His dad was probably another intimacy avoider. Just as a master craftsman teaches his apprentice, his dad likely taught him the proud, honorable trade of holding in feelings and being a poor communicator. He has been carefully trained through years and years of modeling to carry on the family business of building a mediocre marriage.

He probably never—and I mean *never*—saw a significant man in his life share something personal. It just didn't happen. Dad didn't do it. Neither one of his grandpas did it. His brother didn't do it. Uncle Harry didn't do it. None of his male teachers or coaches did. So he learned not to share personal things with other men and certainly not with women.

What he did see, time after time until there were too many times to count, was his dad and other key men in his life choking back their emotions. Stuffing all personal reactions. Refusing to answer personal questions women asked. Saying as little as possible and sticking to the facts. Being logical. Avoiding conflicts. Showing emotion only while watching sports.

He may also have seen his mom and dad develop and maintain a marriage devoid of any real intimacy. It may have been a decent marriage, but not a great one. He saw his mom carry on bravely for years, enabling her husband and acting as though everything was okay with her. In truth, she was unhappy and unfulfilled. But he didn't see his mom's pain.

He thought—and still thinks—his parent's marriage was "fine" or "okay." He actually believes that the relationship they had (and may still have) is as good as marriage gets. He'll say, "They had a good marriage." "They got along." "They never fought." "They built a solid, stable life together." Wonderful. Doesn't sound too exciting and passionate, does it? If his parents got divorced or had some obvious trouble in their marriage, he has no idea why.

No wonder a Caveman can't emotionally connect. All the men in his growing-up years modeled poor communication. He's never seen a man and a woman engage in personal, deep conversation. He's never experienced emotional intimacy with another person. He has no idea what intimacy looks like. He has no idea how to get it. All he knows is how to avoid intimacy. He has those skills down cold because he was trained by the best.

How the Husband Avoids Emotional Intimacy

The vast majority of Cavemen were born and raised to avoid intimacy with other people. Clueless about closeness. Uncomfortable with deep, personal conversations. Geared to get away from any interaction that might lead to emotional connection.

The Caveman is a master of avoiding intimacy. He's been doing it his whole life. Like the Great Houdini, he is a world-class escape artist.

He'll do whatever is necessary to weasel out of a close, deep conversation with his wife. Here are some of his escape-from-closeness tricks:

Answering a Question with a Question

Your wife asks you, "How are you doing?" You respond, "Why do you ask?" She's thinking, *What do you mean, why do I ask? I'm trying to start a conversation. I want to know you better.*

She asks you, "What are you thinking?" You respond with a question that makes no sense: "Who knows?" Your wife is thinking, *Well, I guess the only person who knows would be you.*

Pleading Ignorance

Here is one of your classic escape lines to any question requiring personal information: "I don't know." It is a beautiful, inoffensive way to kill a conversation cold. You're really telling your woman, "I'd love to talk to you, honey, but I have no information. If only I could think of one thing that happened to me today...but I can't. Sorry. My mind's a complete blank." It's amazing how a Caveman knows completely zilch when his wife is trying to get a conversation going. The fact is that you just don't want to talk, and this brain cramp is a wonderful excuse.

Massive Generalizations

Your wife asks, "How was your day?" You answer, "Fine" or "Okay." Too bad you can't build much of a conversation on these two global replies. Of course, that's why you respond this way. You want to give her nothing to work with. You have courteously answered her question and escaped any possibility of closeness. This is like her asking, "Where do you live?" and you responding, "The Milky Way."

No Response

You simply don't respond to her questions. You say absolutely nothing. Like the Great Sphinx in Egypt, your face and body are carved out of stone. Your wife could stick you with a pin—and it's tempting—and you'd give no reaction. She's thinking, *Am I here? Do I exist? Is he in some parallel universe? Did he hear me?* Oh, you heard all right. You're exercising elective mutism. You're letting her know that you don't want to talk about whatever topic she has brought up.

Refusal to Talk

"I don't want to talk about it." How many times have you told your wife that? Or its time-honored corollary, "This isn't a good time to talk?" You're tired, stressed, and too full from dinner. The ball game is coming on, you have a crick in your neck…You seem to indicate that someday, somewhere, you will find a good time to talk. Believe me, your wife won't live that long.

Letting Her Talk All the Time

You're usually happy to let your Cinderella talk. Of course, you're not always listening that closely. If she's talking and filling the air with words, you don't have to talk. A monologue does not create intimacy. Intimacy requires a dialogue, so you avoid it by encouraging her to ramble on alone.

Snap and Then Leave

You get angry, snap some nasty comment at her, and leave the room. You can't simply stand up and leave, so you cleverly create a reason to get out of her conversational clutches. You don't want to leave (yeah, right), but she made you angry, so you have to go. If she gets angry or exasperated—which is perfectly understandable—that plays right into your hands. You'll say she's overreacting, and since you can't talk to an overreactor, you have to leave. And it's her fault!

Drop It and Move On

When she wants to talk through a conflict, you will accuse her of dwelling on the past. You fail to recognize that the past is not the past until you've dealt with it together and come to an understanding. You use statements like "I said I was sorry," or "Stop bringing that up" to end conflict conversations. You believe if she drops the subject, the problem will magically disappear.

You, like most Cavemen, absolutely hate conflict with your wife. You'd rather face a firing squad than work through a conflict with her. Dealing with conflict—for you—is like turning the car around, going back two miles, scraping roadkill off the pavement, and eating it for dinner.

You don't understand that if you ignore or sidestep a conflict, it doesn't go away. It remains, festers, and pushes the two of you further apart. Unintentionally, you are hurting and disrespecting your woman. The unresolved conflict also carries over to the next conflict. So when you fight over the next thing, you're fighting about the current issue *and* all the other unresolved conflicts. So you see, you can't just drop it and move on. You'll drag it along behind you.

Too Busy to Talk

You're a busy, busy man. You've got to do a lot of important things and, sad though it is, that just doesn't leave any time to talk with her. You have to work, watch television, dink around on the computer, do yard work, fix things around the house, read the paper, sleep, or whatever else you can think of to avoid conversation with her.

You're more comfortable doing activities that you enjoy, that help you escape from stress, and that you're good at. Talking with your wife is tough, and you don't feel very competent in this area. So you wimp out of it by staying busy doing things you'd rather do. You're not fooling her. You're breaking her heart.

Can't Talk but Can Have Sex

She starts talking, and you start fondling her. She's trying to connect emotionally, and her conversationally impaired husband is in groping mode! Why waste time talking when you can have sex? When she doesn't respond favorably (what a shocker!), you get offended and accuse her of rejecting you. You're angry and pouty, so of course no one could expect you to talk to her.

You don't realize that her need for emotional connection is just as powerful as your need for sex. And because she cannot respond sexually without the emotional connection, you've got to learn to talk with her and meet her emotional needs *before* sex.

The Logical Man

You bury your emotions and are aware only of cold, hard, rational logic. When your wife expresses her emotions, you don't realize she is being a normal and healthy female—a fully functioning human being. You see her expression as a bizarre, unnecessary, and frightening monster that you must stamp out immediately. You try your logic to talk her out of her feelings. "Honey, you shouldn't feel that way." "Honey, calm down, and let's look at the facts." "Honey, listen up, and I'll tell you how to fix your problem." Of course, your logic infuriates her and hurts her. Conversation over.

Caveman, haven't you noticed how many conversations you kill with your logic? Your wife is emotional and expressing herself about a topic. You come back with a logical response. She gets even more emotional and intense because she needs understanding and not logic. You get frustrated and edgy and defensive because you don't want her to be more emotional. Then…this is not going to end well.

You and your wife will not connect in this conversation. And now you get the added bonus of a woman who is upset. Hurt. Angry. Unhappy. You will now pay the price for your logical responses. And it's your own fault.

The Martyr

When your wife urges you to talk, you'll say in a whiny, pitiful voice, "I guess I can't ever please you." Somehow your refusal to talk becomes your wife's fault because she can't be pleased. You think her expectations are too high. You think she wants too much. You are a poor, dear man who has tried his little heart out, and your very best is just not good enough for her. This clever ruse is nothing more than a distraction from the real issue. Your wife's expectations—that you both talk and share yourselves and your lives—are reasonable. She wants what every wife wants!

The Genetic Excuse

If all else fails, you will resort to these old standards: "Hey, this is who I am." "You knew I was like this when you chose to marry me." "I can't change." Bogus. Bogus. Bogus. This may be who you are, but you don't have to stay that way. Unless you both were freeze-dried right after your wedding and put into cold storage, you both need to change as the marriage progresses. You can change, and you need to if the two of you are going to build an intimate relationship. When people refuse to change, they almost never have wonderful marriages. In fact, their marriages often don't survive. But God is in the business of changing believers' lives.

The Dialogue

Caveman: "Doc, she wants to talk all the time! She's always asking me questions."

Me: "I know. You married a woman. She really wants to know who you are, to be close to you. Don't fight her—let her in!"

Caveman: "I'm a simple guy. All I need is food on the table, sex on a regular basis, and peace at home."

Me: "Spoken like a true Caveman. Your wife needs more than these basic things. Frankly, even though you don't realize it yet, so do you. You both have a God-given need for the emotional connection that comes through deeper conversations."

Caveman: "I don't talk much. I don't have much to say. I guess you could say I'm a man of few words."

Me: "Yeah, your wife has noticed. Look, you

Caveman: "don't have to become some huge talker. You just have to learn to talk and share enough. She'll be happy with that."

Caveman: "When she's upset and emotional, I try to calm her down. But she gets more upset!"

Me: "Ever throw gasoline on a fire? That's what you're doing when you use logic to help her calm down. She doesn't need logic. She needs you to listen, reflect back to her what you're hearing, and understand."

Caveman: "I have no idea how to communicate with her. Nobody ever taught me how to do it."

Me: "That's where I come in. I'm going to teach you how. My strategies have worked for thousands of husbands—in my therapy practice and in my marriage seminars. They'll work for you too."

Goodbye, Great Houdini
Hello, Good Communicator

Does anything in this chapter sound familiar? I'll bet it does. I was guilty of all these communication mistakes with Sandy. That's why I can describe them so well. For the first ten years of our marriage, I didn't have a clue about how to communicate with my wife.

I had to realize that all my intimacy-avoidance techniques were hurting me, Sandy, and our relationship. I wasn't intentionally causing damage and pain. Sidestepping closeness was automatic for me. It's what came naturally. I had no idea I was keeping us from an intimate, joyful life together.

I figured out what I was doing wrong, and with help from God and Sandy, I made the necessary corrections. I still make mistakes, but most of the time I do things right, and that has made all the difference in our communication and in our marriage.

If I can do it, you can do it. Let's get to the how-tos.

Marriage Enrichment Steps

1. Husband, tell your wife about your childhood. How active were you as a boy? What activities did you participate in? Were you a doer or a talker?

2. Husband, describe your dad: his personality, the time he spent with you, and the way he communicated his feelings. What kind of marriage did your dad and mom have as you grew up? How did they communicate, resolve conflicts, and show affection? How are you like your dad?

3. Husband, answer question 2 again, but this time, apply it to your mom.

4. Husband, tell your wife which of the 13 escape-from-closeness tricks you believe you use most often. Ask her which ones you use the most. Ask her to lovingly catch you using these tricks so you can stop doing them.

8

Caveman, Open Up and Talk

Take the Lead, Listen Smart, and Share Personally

All right, Caveman. You married her. Now, you've got to communicate with her. You say, "You've already established the fact that I don't know how to communicate with my wife. I regularly make these 13 mistakes and then some. I need some help here, Doc, so how do I do it?" Well, you've come to the right place. Here's how.

You Are the Man

I'll get right to the point. Caveman, it's your job to lead the way to better communication. In fact, it's your job to lead her in every area of your relationship. I'm not telling you that, God is.

> Wives, be subject to your own husbands, as to the Lord. For the husband is the head of the wife, as Christ also is the head of the church, He Himself being the Savior of the body. But as the church is subject to Christ, so also the wives ought to be to their husbands in everything (Ephesians 5:22-24).

Pretty clear, isn't it? God didn't leave any loopholes when assigning leadership in marriage. If the wife leads in communication, it will never be efficient and successful. It can't! Female leadership is not

God's design. Both of you are to be involved in the communication process, but God wants *you* to lead the way.

Your first duty as communication leader is to create regular times to talk and make sure you have topics to discuss. Remember the 30-minute daily talk times and talk-time schedule from chapter 6? If you haven't read that chapter, read it *right now*. You need this information. Go ahead. Your wife will wait.

Husband, you are responsible to sit down with your wife and schedule at least four 30-minute talk times each week. You are responsible to go to her and say, "It's time for our talk, honey." You are also responsible to post the talk-time schedule and ensure you are using it properly.

You noticed in chapter 6 that your wife can approach you and seek to establish the talk times and talk-time schedule. Very often, the wife has to initially take the lead because the husband won't. Don't force your wife to do it. That is most definitely Plan B. In Plan A, God's plan, you step up and get the job done.

What Do We Talk About?

Husband, you're also in charge of what happens during your couple talk times. I don't mean you'll be the one doing all the talking. You and your wife will both talk, and you will both listen. But *you* will guide the content and flow of the talk times. In other words, as the CEO, you run the meeting and determine the agenda.

Here's your crash course in how to run a couple talk time.

Create Some Ambiance

Meet with your wife in an atmosphere that is warm, soft, and inviting. This is more important to her than it is to you. Make sure the conversation area is clear of empty cups, wrappers, and miscellaneous clutter. Have some low-key music playing in the background, like one of her favorite worship or Christian CDs. Get her a cup of coffee, a mug of tea, or a soft drink. One or two candles burning wouldn't be a bad idea. Offer to give her a neck, back, or foot massage as you sit down and begin the meeting.

A Brief Prayer

Take her hand and say a short prayer. It could be something like this: "Dear Father, thank You for my wonderful wife. Thank You for this time we have together. Please be with us and help us open up and really connect in conversation." This will automatically deepen the mood and help you both prepare to communicate.

Read Your Couple's Devotional

An easy and effective way to kick off communication is to read a page from a couple's devotional book and answer the questions at the end of the page. When you're just starting on your talk times, coming up with conversational material can be difficult. Reading a devotional page is a great conversation starter. My two favorite devotionals for couples are the Dobsons' *Night Light* and the Raineys' *Moments Together for Couples*.

Husband, prepare by reading the devotional page a day or two before the meeting. Being a man, you need time to digest the information and process it. Use a writing pad (remember the pad from chapter 4?) to jot down your comments and reactions. This way, you'll have some things to say, and she'll be impressed that you spent time preparing to talk with her.

You both discuss your reactions to the devotional page and answer the questions at the end. The devotional may trigger a stimulating conversation. Something in the page or in a question may lead to a deeper talk. If you find an interesting topic like this and want to talk about it again, jot it down on your pad. Think about the topic over the next day or so and jot down your impressions and ideas. Then, at the next talk time, you can continue the talk on that topic by sharing what you have on your pad.

Your wife doesn't need a pad. She remembers everything. She'll be impressed that you did some work on the topic, and she will have no trouble jumping right into the conversation.

Carryover Topics

Next, you can segue into revisiting topics of interest you've discussed in previous talk times or in other conversations. This is the carryover principle I explained in chapter 6: talking about the same topic two, three, or four times to achieve a deeper level of emotional intimacy.

Whether you bring up one of these carryover topics or your wife does, you can say, "Yes, the pastor's sermon. We talked about that on Monday and agreed to continue that talk today. I thought more about it, and I wrote down some things that came into my head."

Without the pad, you'll sit there like the village idiot with absolutely nothing to say. "What? The sermon? Are you sure we talked about that? I forgot what the sermon was about, and I'm fuzzy on our talk about it." With the pad, you'll sit there like a man who cares enough about his wife to remember topics of conversation and actually prepare to talk more about them.

You'll go from a Caveman to a caring conversationalist. The Caveman gets disappointment, disgust, no respect, no intimacy, and mediocre sex. The caring conversationalist gets warmth, love, emotional intimacy, respect, and better and more frequent sex. So who do you want to be?

If both of you decide to continue talking about a carryover topic, jot it on your pad and put it on the talk-time schedule.

Current Events

After getting a little deeper into one or two carryover topics, you can bring up new material: work, kids, home maintenance, social plans, friends and family, church, and events of interest that have occurred since your last talk time.

If any of these prove stimulating and promise more intimacy, agree to carry them over to the next talk time. Jot these topics down on your pad for processing and write them on the talk-time schedule.

Prayer Together

Make a list of prayer requests on a pad. You can call this your prayer pad. Divide up the list and pray out loud, one at a time, for the items on the list. Make sure you hold her hand during this five-minute prayer time. If you're in a crisis or have a pressing concern, you'll pray for more than five minutes. Remember to thank God for who He is, His many blessings, and His presence and help in your talk time.

Prayer to Conversation

When you finish praying, you will naturally talk about some of the issues you just lifted up to God. These are the concerns of your heart, and following up on them with conversation can lead to real emotional intimacy.

One more time to make sure you get it: If you agree to keep talking about any topic that comes up during your talk time, jot it down *immediately* on your pad and put it down *immediately* on the talk-time schedule. Keep the talk-time schedule with you during the talk time.

This progression I've explained is not set in concrete. It has, however, proven very helpful to many couples who are beginning the talk-time program. It provides some structure, a nice flow, and multiple opportunities for deeper conversations. Try it and see how it goes. Play with the order of steps and mix it up to find a sequence that works best for you and your wife. Every now and then, change the order to keep things fresh.

Conversational intimacy is unpredictable, so in every talk time, the sequence of steps is subject to sudden change. If you hit a winning topic and you are building an interesting conversation, go with it. Following a potentially intimate conversational branch is more important than covering all the steps in the talk-time progression.

Now, let's go a little deeper into the specific areas of listening and talking to your woman. These principles will apply to the talk times and to conversations that occur at other times.

Listen Smart

Listening to your wife in a smart way is a critical part of good communication. If you listen in a dumb way, you'll kill the communication. She has to know that you get it, that you grasp what she's saying and feeling. This understanding is the first essential link in the chain of conversation.

Before I explain the how-tos, here are the benefits of listening smart:

- You'll build understanding.
- She'll talk less.
- She'll come down in emotional intensity.
- She'll feel closer to you.
- She'll feel loved.
- You'll get warmed up and into the conversation.
- You'll be able to share more personally.
- She'll be ready to listen to what you have to say.
- She'll be happy.

The consequences of listening dumb are just the opposite:

- You'll create no understanding.
- She'll talk more.
- She'll go up in emotional intensity.
- She'll feel more distant from you.
- She'll feel unloved.
- You won't warm up and will stay out of the conversation.
- You won't be able to share more personally.
- She won't want to listen to what you have to say.
- She'll be unhappy.

The stakes are high, Caveman. Very high. You need to learn to listen smart. Here's how.

Be an Active Listener

Listening smart means being an active listener. When she opens her beautiful mouth to speak, allow no distractions. Establish eye contact. Lock on to her just as a missile locks on to its target. As she speaks, you verbally feed back her content (what she is saying) and her emotion (what she is feeling about what she is saying). You don't repeat everything she says. Just repeat key words and phrases so she knows you're understanding her message:

> Caveman: "Boy, you had a lot of fun at the beach. Except for that dumb parking attendant, you and your girlfriends had a great time. You felt relaxed and close to your friends."
>
> Caveman: "That nurse at the doctor's office was way out of line. I can't believe how she treated you. Talk about rude! I don't blame you for being furious."
>
> Caveman: "I'm sorry your dad treated you so badly. What an insensitive jerk! I can see you're angry and sad. I don't know why he can't be proud of you and all you've accomplished."

As you feed back her content and emotion, ask her periodically if she feels understood:

> "Do you feel I'm understanding what you're saying and feeling?"
>
> "Do you feel I'm getting it?"
>
> "Are you angry or more frustrated?"
>
> "Do you feel I'm with you in this conversation?"

You need to actively listen regardless of what she is saying and feeling. You must actively listen even when she's saying something you consider trivial. When she's emotionally intense. When she seems unreasonable, irrational, or isn't making any sense. When she's convinced she's right. When she jumps from topic to topic, following a whole series of conversational rabbit trails. When she changes her mind.

You also need to actively listen when she repeats herself. When a woman talks, she'll repeat a story three or four times. That's the way she figures out her emotions and determines how to react to what happened to her. If you actively listen, she will talk less. But she'll still repeat herself. You must hang in there and stay in active listening mode.

Always, always, always, actively listen to her first. Later, after she feels understood, you can share the original things you have to say: your point of view, your perspective, and your opinion.

Be Captivated by Her Talking

Every woman, including yours, wants her husband to be captivated by her. The deep desire of her heart is for her man to find her irresistible, fascinating, and interesting. Read these words Solomon spoke to his sweetie:

> Let me see your form,
>
> Let me hear your voice;
>
> For your voice is sweet,
>
> And your form is lovely (Song of Solomon 2:14).

Solomon wanted to hear her talk. He was hanging on her every word! He was attracted to her physical beauty and also to her conversation. The Shulammite woman was thrilled by Solomon's attention and loved him right back.

So be like Solomon and enjoy the show when your wife is talking. Her expressiveness, spontaneity, emotional intensity, and unpredictable conversational style is very entertaining. If she talked like you—logically, without many words and without much emotion—the two of you would be bored to death. Thank God every day that she is a woman and talks like a woman.

Relive Her Story

Allow yourself—push yourself—to be emotionally drawn into the story she is telling. She doesn't need you to be a mere observer, standing outside and watching her tell her story. She needs you to be a participant, reliving her story right alongside her. When she's describing an event, here's what she's thinking:

See what happened to me?

Do you feel what I felt going through it?

Do you understand what it was like for me?

I want you to know me better because you walked through this experience with me.

This kind of "walk in her shoes, feel what she's feeling" empathy is not one of your strong points. She's a lot better at it than you are. But you can do it. When you watch an action-adventure movie, you get into the story, don't you? You feel emotions, and you can relate to the hero as he kills the bad guys, fights past the obstacles, and rescues the woman, right? Of course you do. Your challenge is to react and respond in these same ways to your wife when she's telling a story about an event in her life.

One of the key ways to relive events with your wife is to mirror her emotions as she's talking. Work hard to feel what she is feeling. Don't just feed back and understand her emotion; actually feel some of it yourself. This is Romans 12:15 in action: "Rejoice with those who rejoice, and weep with those who weep."

If she's angry, you're angry. And you let her see your anger. If she's sad, you're sad. If she's frustrated, you're frustrated. If she's happy, you're happy. You won't feel 100 percent of what she's feeling because you're not her. And you're not that good at empathetic listening. Work at this and do your best. You'll get better at it with practice.

Another way to relive her events and feel connected to her is to ask specific questions about the details of her story. This shows interest and helps draw you into her story. Zero in on the aspects of her story that interest you and ask questions:

"What did you say when the parking guy spit on the ground?"

"What did that nurse look like?"

"How old was that nurse?"

"What did you want to say to your dad after he criticized you?"

"Did your mom say anything after his comments? I mean, she was sitting right there!"

If You Can't Listen, Tell Her

Sometimes you are not prepared to actively listen to your wife. You're far better off telling her that right up front than doing a poor listening job and making her feel angry, hurt, and disgusted. Maybe you're tired. Preoccupied. Stressed. Angry. Sick. Right at the end of an exciting sporting event on television.

Say something like this: "Honey, I'm sorry, but I can't listen to you now. I'm not in the right frame of mind. I'm (whatever the reason is). Let's schedule a time right now to talk about it, okay?" Schedule the time and put it on your pad and in your Day-Timer or PDA so you don't forget. If it's going to be part of your next talk time, put it on the talk-time schedule.

You Must Talk to Her

Leading her by scheduling talk times and overseeing the use of the talk-time schedule is important. Guiding the content and flow of your talk times is important. Listening smart is important. What you say to her and how you say it is also important.

Tell a Story with Details

When you're telling her about something that happened to you, force yourself to be more detailed. Don't give her just the broad, general sketch: "I had a good day." "I had a bad day." "Work was okay." "The interview went fine." "I've had better days." "Work is work." What do these comments tell her? Nothing!

She needs to know you so she can get closer to you. To meet this need, you must share the events of your day in more detail: what happened, how it happened, where it happened, when it happened, why you think it happened, who was involved, and how you feel about what happened.

When in doubt, tell her more. This is like doing a complicated math problem. You can just give the final answer, or you can show the work you did to get to the answer. Show her your work. You'll never be as detailed and descriptive as she is, but do your best.

Being logical is okay at first. That's who you are and how your mind works. After your logical—and as detailed as possible—sharing, take the time to process what you've said and find your emotional, personal reaction to it. Jot the topic on your pad, put it on the talk-time schedule, and carry the topic over into your next talk time.

As you process for a day or two, let yourself go emotionally. Allow yourself to feel the raw, intense emotions connected to the event you told her about in the first conversation. Drop your brave, macho, logical front and dig up your feelings.

First talk:	Give the details of a confrontation with your boss at work. What happened, what people said, what they did, and the like.
Processing:	Think about the confrontation and pray that God will help you identify and feel your emotions. Jot down what you feel on your pad.
Second talk:	"Honey, I've been processing that confrontation with my boss. He had no right to treat me that way. I'm angry and feel betrayed. Used. I'm discouraged. I'm also scared because I wonder if I'm going to lose my job. It reminds me of how my dad used to treat me and…"

Here are some conversational topics that have a pretty good chance to lead to emotional connection and intimacy with your wife:

1. An event that triggered strong emotions, whether positive (such as happiness, relief, or joy) or difficult (like anger, frustration, rage, despair, discouragement, or hurt).

2. A stressful situation or interaction with someone that you experienced.

3. Any comment or question about your marriage: "How are we doing as a couple?" "Do you feel close to me this week?" "You seem distant these last few days—what's going on?" "Am I meeting your needs this week?"

4. Spiritual issues: how you are doing in your relationship with God, what you're learning in your quiet times this week, what you're learning in your Bible study at church, or how God is guiding you lately. Ask her to comment on these same spiritual areas in her life.

Husband, as you go through your day, jot down topics like these on your pad. Think about them and also jot down what comes to mind. Then share what's on your pad at the next talk time.

Marriage Enrichment Steps

1. Husband, do you believe you are responsible to lead your wife in the area of communication? Will you agree to lead by creating regular talk times each week and supervising the use of the talk-time schedule? What obstacles will you have to overcome to lead in this way?

2. Right now, schedule your four talk times for this week. Also, create a talk-time schedule and post it.

3. Husband, what do you think (and feel) about my description of a talk time? Which steps will be easier to do, and which ones will be harder for you?

4. Husband, tell your wife what kind of listener you think you are. Now, ask her what kind of listener she thinks you are. Which of the listening principles in this chapter are you willing to practice?

5. Husband, which of the talking principles are you willing to apply? Will you use a pad to jot down topics to process, and will you share those topics with your wife?

6. At the end of each talk time during the next month, take a few minutes and discuss how the time went: what worked, what didn't work, and how you can both improve your communication skills.

9

Cinderella, You're Too Focused on the Kids and the Home

Make Your Husband Number One

Read these snapshots of seven wives with whom I've talked in my therapy office during the past month. Each wife describes, in her own words, one particular area of her life. See if you recognize yourself in one or more of these stories.

Homework Helper

"Dr. Clarke, you would not believe the time I have to spend every night with my son helping him do his homework. The schools these days just load it on! We sit down at three p.m., and I don't leave his side, except for short breaks, until five! We eat dinner as a family, and then we often have to spend another forty-five minutes to an hour finishing it all up.

"I'm glad I can be there for him because he needs my help. No, he doesn't have any learning disabilities. He's bright, but he has trouble focusing and really applying himself. On his own, I just know he wouldn't turn in excellent work. Our work does pay off. We're—I mean, he—is on the honor roll every grading period.

"Math and science aren't too bad, but what I find the most difficult are the written reports and essays for English. I'm a better writer than he is, so I give him a lot of help. Well, okay, I write almost all the papers for him. What I find very tricky is writing in such a way that the teacher believes it's his words. I'll make mistakes in grammar and spelling on purpose to make it look like the work of an elementary school student. It's amazing the lengths you have to go to when you're a mom!"

Date Killer

"You want to know why we hardly ever go out on dates as a couple? I'll tell you why. I don't like leaving my kids, even for a few hours. I guess it's a mom thing. I worry about them a lot, and I'm a nervous wreck those few times a year we do leave them at home with someone else. I mean, what if something went wrong and they needed their mom? I just couldn't forgive myself if that happened.

"We had kids so we could be a family. I love being with them. Leaving them doesn't make sense, especially when they're small. A babysitter wouldn't treat them the way I do. A babysitter wouldn't know what they like to eat, what games they like to play, or how to comfort them if they get upset.

"Speaking of babysitters, finding one I can trust my kids to is almost impossible. A teenage girl isn't up to the job, and college girls are usually too busy. And unless I know a babysitter really well, how could I be confident she would keep my babies safe? No, I can't take the chance. I will only leave my kids with my parents. How often do they visit us? Twice a year."

Sleeping Beauty

"Every night around eight, I put my daughter in bed. I lie down next to her, and we talk, pray, play little games, listen to music, and make up stories. How long do I stay with her? Well, that depends on her. She can't go to sleep on her own, so I stay until she drops off. It usually takes thirty minutes to an hour.

"Most nights, I drop off to sleep before she does. It's dark in there, and I'm tired. On some nights, I'll sleep with her until my husband wakes me up to come to bed with him. On other nights, I'll only sleep for a little while before I leave her room. I'm so groggy and out of it, though, that I'm not much use to anyone the rest of the evening.

"My husband thinks I'm going overboard by sleeping with her. But I know she can't get to sleep without me. He wants me to put her to bed much more quickly and leave her by herself. How cruel! She and I look forward to our routine."

Professional Housekeeper

"I've been told I'm a perfectionist, and I suppose that's true. It's just who I am. My husband doesn't understand my need to keep my home clean and orderly. There are so many jobs, and they all have to be done, don't they? Laundry, dishes, vacuuming, cleaning the bathrooms, dusting, making sure the kids' rooms are in good shape, and on and on. I remember my mom working for hours every evening on household jobs.

"I can't relax each evening until all the jobs are done. I've always been that way. My husband tells me to lighten up and not to do all the jobs. I can't do that because I know those jobs will be waiting for me tomorrow. Besides, I'm responsible to take care of the home. If something isn't done and done right, it reflects on me."

Big Momma, Big Mouth

"I'm sick and tired of having to do practically all of the work around our home. I thought slavery was abolished. I work all day, and then I have to come home and work for a few more hours doing household chores. Yeah, I guess you could say I'm bitter about it.

"My husband is lazy and irresponsible. I tell him that on a regular basis, not that it does any good. He parks his rear end on the recliner and keeps it there all night. I nag him constantly to do chores. I hate being so critical and sarcastic, but that's the only way I can get him to do anything. I tell him all the time he's just like one of the kids. I feel like his mother, not his wife."

Never Home

"I tell you, being a mom is like having two full-time jobs. It's not so much the jobs at home that drive me crazy, it's all the kid-related activities outside the home. I cart the kids to dance, gymnastics, sports, church meetings, birthday parties, and so on. I'm on the PTA, I'm the home-room mom for one of my kids, I teach a Sunday school class, and I'm on two committees at church.

"My husband says I'm too busy and I'm never home. I tell him this is what a mom's life is all about. Most of the moms I know are doing just as much as I am. I want to be a good mom and do all I can to help my kids be happy, have friends, and succeed in life. I tell my husband our turn will come when the kids leave home."

Sorry, No Sex

"Ever since I became a mom, my sex drive has gone way down. Most of the time I think about my kids and what they need. I don't see myself as a wife and a sexual person anymore. I see myself as a...well, a mom. I'm too busy for sex. My career, the kids and all the work they require, and the never-ending household chores tire me out. Frankly, I'm exhausted every night, and the last thing I want to do is have sex. I just don't have the energy for one more job.

"I also can't have sex if any of the kids are awake. I don't feel com-fortable because I'm afraid they might know what we're doing. I don't want them to hear anything. When we do have sex, it's late at night when all the kids are finally asleep. I'm afraid by this time I'm exhausted and probably not too responsive. What's that? Yes, you're right. Falling asleep in the middle of sex doesn't do much to boost my husband's ego."

The Dialogue

Homework Helper: "I want my child to succeed. Is that a crime?"

Me: "Actually, what you're doing *is* a crime. It's a crime against your son because you're car-rying him. He's in school, not you! You're teaching him dependence, not indepen-dence. Do you plan to room with him in college so you can continue to help him?

But the real crime is against your husband. You're robbing him of your time, energy, and attention."

Date Killer: "I can't trust anyone to babysit. My mom didn't leave us with babysitters. We can date when the kids are older."

Me: "You can find trustworthy sitters in your church or neighborhood. Or trade off babysitting duties with other couples. Your mom was wrong not to use babysitters. Bring her in here, and I'll tell her she was wrong. If you wait until your kids are older, it may be too late. You need dates to create romance and passion."

Sleeping Beauty: "If I don't sleep with her, she won't sleep. My husband doesn't understand."

Me: "Baloney. She can so sleep without you. Your bedtime wimpiness is keeping her from learning to sleep on her own. Put her in bed, spend five minutes with her, and leave. Lock her in her room if you have to. She'll scream her living guts out for a few nights, and then she'll get the hang of it. Your husband understands just fine. He understands your daughter is more important to you than he is. He feels rejected, and I don't blame him."

Professional Housekeeper: "The jobs have to be done! I want my home to be neat and clean."

Me: "Yes, the jobs have to be done, but not all in the same day. And not before you give your husband some attention. Why does your home have to be perfect? Is the queen of England coming over every evening? Congratulations. You've got a clean home and a lousy marriage. Please show me where the Bible says taking care of the home is

	more important than taking care of your husband."
Big Momma, Big Mouth:	"He needs criticism. I have to be hard on him so he'll take action."
Me:	"There are better ways to motivate him. He needs your respect, not your criticism and belittling comments. No man likes being treated like a boy. You're not his mother. You are emasculating him and pushing him further and further away."
Never Home:	"I don't mind sacrificing for my kids. I don't need a life."
Me:	"You may not need a life, but your husband needs a wife. You are way overcommitted and need to cut back. Let's practice saying the word *no*."
Sorry, No Sex:	"I can do without sex. I don't want to traumatize the kids by letting them know we're having sex."
Me:	"You actually do need sex, and so does your husband. You're robbing yourself and him of this wonderful gift from God. You're traumatizing your husband by denying him sex! Sex is to be a pleasurable, joyful, fun, stress-releasing, and loving act that regularly unites the two of you. God wants it to occur as often as possible. And it's okay for the kids to know you're having sex. Of course, it is a very private, intimate experience, and there are easy ways to ensure that they hear nothing."

Your Priorities Are out of Whack

Admittedly, once you become a mom, your life is never the same. And by nature, you (and most women) have a powerful internal drive to keep your home clean and orderly. But neither your children nor your home are your top human priority.

I told all seven of these wives that they had their priorities mixed up. They were shocked to hear that. They were even more shocked when I said they were unintentionally hurting their marriages. Their husbands felt neglected and rejected. Their husbands were cold, distant, not romantic, and not pursuing them in communication. And I told them they were part of the problem.

All these wives explained that they really had no choice but to focus on their kids and their homes. That's just the way it had to be. They said if I were a woman, I'd understand. I responded that I wasn't speaking from my own wisdom but from the wisdom of God. To make my case for their poor priorities, I took them to the Bible.

Husbands Are Number One

A quick walk through the Bible reveals that a wife's number one human priority is her husband.

Genesis 2:18. The wife is called a "helper." The Hebrew term means she is designed to meet her husband's needs. The husband has needs that only his wife can meet. This verse also makes it clear that the man is not complete without his wife. How can you help him and complete him if you're neglecting him?

Genesis 2:24. "One flesh" describes a complete union of a husband and a wife physically, emotionally, and spiritually. It is a sacred, unique relationship that occurs only in marriage. You are not one flesh with your kids, your home, your job, or anyone or anything else.

Proverbs 31:10-31. This magnificent, almost too-good-to-be-true wife was a very busy woman. But she did not neglect her husband. He was very happy with her. In fact, she performed all of her many jobs *for* her husband. This section of Scripture is often titled The Excellent Wife, not The Excellent Mother or The Excellent Housekeeper.

The Song of Solomon. The Shulammite woman was crazy about her husband, Solomon, and she kept up this intense focus on him throughout their entire marriage. She consistently gave him exactly what he needed: attention, romantic love, touch, and respect. She treated him like a king. Of course, he was the king, but you get the idea. Your husband is your king.

1 Peter 3:1-2,6. Peter instructs wives to respect their husbands. This means to hold them in high honor and esteem. Sarah actually called Abraham *lord.* I wouldn't recommend using that word, but do cultivate the attitude of respect that word implies.

Ephesians 5:33. At the end of this powerful passage on marriage, Paul exhorts wives to "see to it" that they respect their husbands.

Titus 2:4-5. When Paul is providing practical guidance for young wives, what is the very first word of instruction he gives? What comes *first* in the chain of commands in this passage? Here's what: "love their husbands." *Second,* women are to love their children. *Fifth,* he mentions taking care of the home.

Work as a Team with Kids and Housework

I think I've made my point that your first priority is to be a wife, to focus on your husband's needs *before* the kids and the home and your career. Here's how to do it.

Even if your husband is the laziest man alive and is no help with the kids and housework, you can still take some action to make him your number one human priority. But obviously, you will be able to do a better job focusing on him if he does his share in these important areas.

Chapters 3 and 4 give husbands significant guidance in meeting their wives' needs. Some of those same principles can be applied to this situation, and here are several additional steps I recommend.

First, sit down with your husband and tell him you have been guilty of neglecting him. You intend to work hard at putting him first and meeting his needs. To do this successfully, though, you need him to be a team player in dealing with the kids, the housework, and other responsibilities. If you and he work together to complete these jobs, you will have more time and energy to devote to him. The more he contributes to the cause, the better life at home will be for him.

Second, discuss the various ways you can be a better team. Invite him to choose from these three daily options from which to choose:

1. The two of you team up during the day and early evening to get a number of jobs done, make time together to meet needs, and then team up again to finish the remaining jobs.

2. You and he make time together first, whether in the morning or lunchtime or soon after the workday in the early evening. Then, together you complete the jobs that must be done.

3. You and he do the necessary jobs first, during the day and initial part of the evening, and then make time together to focus on each other and meet needs.

I've known couples who have teamed up in each of these ways and have been successful. Of course, you and your husband can develop any system that works for your marriage. Keep in mind that your kids need to do their share. Also, follow these guidelines: Ask often what your partner's needs are, communicate your needs clearly, write down the jobs and needs, and post a list of what must be accomplished each day.

You will probably have to spend time with your man and meet his needs before all the kid and home jobs are done. Bite the bullet, be patient, and let these unfinished jobs wait while you focus on your husband.

Give Him Attention

Your Caveman needs attention. Your attention. He can't feel loved without it. Your regularly scheduled talk times (at least four per week, remember?) will meet part of his need for attention. But you can take two other significant actions.

First, join him as often as you can in activities *he* finds enjoyable. This kind of companionship is what nearly every husband craves. Golf, tennis, hunting, fishing, bowling, in-line skating, walking, hiking, bike riding, throwing a Frisbee, cooking, watching television, going to the movies, attending sporting events, playing cards, playing board games, playing video games...

Second, listen to him talk about his job, his hobby, his golf outing with the boys, and how he performed a fix-it job for you around the home. These aren't the most interesting topics in the world, but he's your husband, and listening to him will give him the attention he needs.

Give Him Respect

Every husband has a deep need for his wife's respect. We've already seen what Scripture says about respecting your man (Ephesians 5:33; 1 Peter 3:1-2,6). You can meet this need in two primary ways.

First, do not criticize, belittle, or nag him. These verbal slaps are not merely ineffective motivators, they are damaging, disrespectful barbs that strike at the heart of his manhood. When you cut him verbally or remind him over and over to do something, you are acting like the "contentious woman" Solomon talks about in Proverbs:

> It is better to live in a corner of a roof than in a house shared with a contentious woman (21:9).

That's exactly where your smart, feisty mouth will drive him: to the corner of the roof.

When you have something difficult to say to your Caveman, say it the right way: in private, adult to adult, firmly and honestly, without sarcasm or personal attacks. If you're angry, express that anger clearly and concisely without being mean. As Scripture teaches, speak the truth in love (Ephesians 4:15). To deal with difficult, painful topics and to ask him to do certain chores, use the one-way communication approach from chapter 6.

Second, praise your Caveman often. To get a good picture of how to praise him and how often, read the Song of Solomon. The Shulammite woman showed her deep respect for Solomon by praising him frequently. When I say frequently, I mean frequently. Be like the

Shulammite, and your husband will feel respected. And he'll be motivated to love you in the ways you want to be loved.

Praise him for who he is, for his character, for working at his job, for jobs he does around the home, for spending time with the children, for his physical attractiveness (see "young stag" in Song of Solomon 2:9,17; 8:14), for his efforts to communicate with you, for his spirituality, for his efforts to lead you and the family spiritually...At a bare minimum, praise him for a specific quality or behavior every day. Two or three compliments per day would be even better.

Give Him Food

Your Caveman loves food. It's not just a physical need either. When you feed him well, he feels loved by you. He will be emotionally drawn to you, the one who feeds him. His stomach and his heart are connected.

I know this sounds crude and simplistic, but we are talking about a Caveman. Keep his favorite snacks stocked. Be willing to go to his kind of restaurant at least on every other date. Make as many home-cooked meals as your schedule will allow. Ask him what he'd like for these meals.

Give Him Touch

Just about every husband I've ever talked to wants and needs more physical affection from his wife. More sex too, but I'll save that topic for another chapter. Your Caveman needs you to touch him on a daily basis. I'm talking about significant nonsexual touching: kissing, hugging, neck and foot and back massages, running your fingers through his hair, scalp massages, and making out on the couch or in the bedroom.

Touch communicates love to him and builds up his masculine self-esteem. Touching him can also lower his walls and help him open up in your talk times. When Sandy gives me a five-minute foot massage at the beginning of a talk time, I'm putty in her hands. I feel her love,

I feel relaxed and confident, and I feel like listening better and talking more.

I've seen wives who give more affection and better hugs and kisses to their pets than to their husbands! You might say you're just not an affectionate person. I say, Fine. Get over it. Work hard at being affectionate at least once a day with your husband. It's not optional. He needs your physical touch.

Marriage Enrichment Steps

1. Cinderella, ask your Caveman if he feels like a priority in your life. Ask him who or what he feels is higher than he is on your list of priorities.

2. Cinderella, which of the seven scenarios can you relate to the most (homework helper, date killer, and so forth)? Tell your husband why you tend to focus too much on the kids, the housework, or other activities.

3. Discuss with your husband the system you will use together to handle the kids and the housework as a team.

4. Ask your husband what you can do, specifically, to make him your number one human priority. Which of the male needs (attention, respect, food, and touch) is the most important to him? How can you meet that need every day?

5. Give him permission to catch you when your priorities are out of whack and he feels neglected. Pray with him right now and tell the Lord you will work to prioritize him and meet his needs.

10

Caveman, You're Not Connected to Your Kids

To Be a Better Husband, Be a Better Father

One day, three married women came to see me at my therapy office. Each talked about her husband, the father of her children. At the end of the day, I realized that all three of these women had pinpointed a main weakness in fathers.

First woman: "Dave, my husband is hardly ever home. During the week, he leaves very early in the morning and gets home late at night. He's a workaholic and is completely focused on his career. He brings work home and often works on Saturdays. He often sees the kids for only a few minutes a day. He could be a great father, but the kids and I will never know because he's not around."

Second woman: "My husband does a good job of getting home from work. He watches his schedule and is home with us a good deal of the time. The trouble is, he's present—I mean he's in the house—but he's really not home. He's preoccupied and caught up in his own interests. He has the television on, he's reading the paper, he's on the computer, he's working on projects around the home…He doesn't play with the kids. He doesn't talk to them. The kids and I joke that we have a cardboard-cutout dad, but it's really not too funny."

Third woman: "Dave, my husband is very good at playing with the kids. He'll throw the ball, play board games, and horse around with them in the yard. I appreciate it. The problem is that I have to do everything else for the kids. I make their meals, I clean up after them, I wash their clothes, I get them to school, I help with homework, I discipline them, I take care of birthdays and special events, and I talk to them about personal and spiritual things. I'm tired of carrying the load. I want some help!"

What weakness do all three of these stories illustrate? The uninvolved father: the father who has no personal relationship with his children. I believe most fathers struggle in this area. I know I do.

When Momma Ain't Happy…

After seeing these three ladies, I was able to speak to each of their husbands. We sat in my office and talked about the connection between fathering skills and marriage.

All three Cavemen told me that their wives were unhappy. Their women were cold, edgy, and distant. I told them they were victims of that old and very true adage, "When Momma ain't happy, ain't nobody happy." And then I told each of them, in the nicest way I could, that they had no one to blame but themselves. I told them each something like this:

When your wife became a mom, her life changed forever. From the moment of conception (or adoption), she was bonded—heart and soul—to each child. She will do whatever is necessary to make sure her children are physically, emotionally, and spiritually healthy. She is acutely sensitive to her children's needs and can literally feel what they feel. When they're happy and joyful, so is she. When they suffer, she suffers right along with them.

Here's my point: Every mom needs her husband to love her kids and build a close relationship with each of them. She instinctively knows that a good, connected relationship with Dad is vital to a child's well-being and healthy development.

When you neglect your kids, you strike at your wife's heart. She'll be deeply wounded. Angry at you. Hurt. Sad. Resentful. She'll lose respect for you. She'll lose love for you. She'll pull away from you—not all at once, but gradually.

I've never heard a mom say, "My husband isn't personally involved with my kids, but that's okay. I don't care. I love him more and more anyway." No way. A mom *cannot* separate your relationship with her children from your relationship with her. You might as well ask her to cut out her heart and live without it.

Straight Talk to Dads

Caveman dad, great relationships with your kids are critical, foundational prerequisites to a great relationship with your wife. If you're not close to your kids, you have no chance to get close to your wife and meet her needs. As a mom, she cannot accept and adjust to your poor fathering. It will always be a wedge between you. Always.

As I explained in the previous chapter, wives give more than enough time and attention to the kids and tend to short their husbands. Wives need to peel themselves off the kids and focus more on their husbands. Husbands give more than enough time and attention to their jobs and other interests and tend to short their kids. Husbands need to peel themselves off their careers and hobbies and focus more on the home.

When you meet your kids' needs and build a close relationship with each of them, you meet one of your wife's deepest needs. She'll be happy, she'll feel loved by you, she'll feel close to you, and she'll be much more willing to meet your needs.

The Dialogue

Caveman: "I'm doing just fine as a dad! I think I'm a good father. I love my kids."

Me: "No, you're not doing fine. You wouldn't be sitting here in a shrink's office if you were doing fine. I know you love your kids. The problem is that they don't feel loved by you. Your other problem is that your wife is not happy with your fathering, and that's causing her to pull away from you. Ask her to evaluate your job performance as a dad, and believe what she says."

Caveman: "My job is important to me. It's how I get most of my self-esteem and confidence."

Me: "Your job is important, and God wants you to do it to the best of your ability. But it's not as important as your family. Your wife and kids can meet a much higher percentage of your needs if you'll give them a chance."

Caveman: "I'm working hard to build something that will last at my company. I want to leave a lasting legacy."

Me: "Your most important legacy is not your job, it's your children. Fifty years from now, people won't be sitting around the office talking about how much you meant to the company. Your kids don't care what you do for a living. To them, you're just Dad. My young son, William, said the other day in a very sarcastic tone, 'He calls himself Dr. David Clarke.' To him, I'm not a psychologist. I'm his dad!"

Caveman: "Look, you don't understand my job. If I say no, I could be fired."

Me: "So be it. God will protect you and bless you for setting limits and focusing on your family. If you are fired, God will give you a better job."

Caveman: "I have a child who doesn't like to do any of the things I like to do."

Me: "So what? It's not about you. Do what the child wants to do, regardless of what it is. Do you think I played with Barbies for years because I like playing with Barbies? I had three little girls, and that's what they wanted to do."

Caveman: "I have a stepchild I can't get along with. We clash all the time. She hates my guts, and I'm not wild about her either."

Me: "Your responsibility before God and your wife is to never stop trying to build a relationship with your stepchild. Did you hear me? Never stop trying. Pray for patience and guidance, ask your wife for ideas, and keep pursuing that kid. Even if you get no response, your wife will appreciate your effort and love you for it."

Caveman: "I have to make a certain amount of money to meet my family's needs. My wife complains about my hours on the job, but she sure likes our lifestyle."

Me: "I'll bet she'd downsize to have you home more often and more involved with her and the kids."

Caveman: "My dad and I weren't all that close. He didn't model good fathering. I really don't know how to build a close relationship with my kids."

Me: "I know how, and I'm going to teach you."

The Bible and Dads

When you're a good father, you personally benefit, your children benefit, and your marriage benefits. These are good reasons to get personally involved with your children. But the best reason of all is that *God* wants you to.

> You shall love the LORD your God with all your heart and with all your soul and with all your might. These words, which I am commanding you today, shall be on your heart. You shall teach them diligently to your sons and shall talk of them when you sit in your house and when you walk by the way and when you lie down and when you rise up (Deuteronomy 6:5-7).

God gave His laws to Moses. Moses passed them on to parents. The parents' job (ultimately, the fathers' job) was to teach the laws to their children. To teach in the active, lifestyle way these verses indicate, the father must be involved with his kids.

> He must be one who manages his own household well, keeping his children under control with all dignity (1 Timothy 3:4).

Male leaders in the church must personally oversee and manage their families. All men ought to aspire to leadership, so I believe this verse speaks to all dads. Fathers are responsible for keeping children under control. This is our job, dads, and we can't do it from a distance.

> Fathers, do not provoke your children to anger, but bring them up in the discipline and instruction of the Lord (Ephesians 6:4).

The words "bring them up" mean to nourish them and meet their needs. Why doesn't Paul direct this verse to moms? Because moms don't need to be told to do what comes naturally. We have to *work* at this nourishing business, dads. How can we nourish our kids and meet their needs if we don't know them intimately? We can't!

The Four *T*s

To develop a close, personal relationship with your children, you must do the four *T*s. If you live with your children full-time, you'll be able to do these behaviors every day. If you're divorced or separated and don't live with your children full-time, you can still do the *T*s when you're with them.

Time

For children of all ages, love is measured in time. Dad, what your children want and need from you more than anything else is your time. How much time? As much as you can possibly give. You can't give too much time, but you can give too little.

You must give your time *first* because without time, you have no personal relationship.

I'm talking about individual, one-on-one time with each child. Specifically, spend five to ten minutes (at a minimum) every day with each child. This is a brief time of personal connection. You can play a game, read a book, pray together, or just talk.

I usually create this time at the end of the day. At bedtime, I spend a few minutes with each of my kids. We talk about how their day went, how they're doing in school, and any problems they're having. We might play something for a few minutes and then have a short prayer.

Periodic playtime is also important. Every two or three weeks, take each child out for a one-on-one activity with Dad. Spend at least an hour or an hour and a half. This is a great way to communicate love and build relationship.

Do whatever the child wants to do in these playtimes. I take my girls to lunch. I go to the bookstore with Emily. I walk the neighborhood with Leeann. I play tennis with Nancy. I play golf with William.

Take advantage of every opportunity to spend a little time with your kids. Drive them to or from school. Invite them along when you're running errands. Help them with their homework. Do chores with them. Every minute counts.

Don't even bother telling me, "I don't have time for these ideas." I'm as busy as you are, and I have four kids. If I can make the time, you can make the time. You have a small window of opportunity with your kids. Seize it and spend time with them.

Touch

Touch feels good. It's warm and personal. It connects two persons. It communicates love. Children of all ages need to be touched on a daily basis. Dad, don't let a day go by without touching each of your children: a squeeze of the shoulder, a pat on the head, a hug, a kiss, a neck rub…

Touching gets trickier the older a child gets, but kids still need it. A teenager won't walk up to you, hold out his arms, and say, "Hold me for a minute." You have to sneak up behind a teen and give a quick touch before he knows what's happening.

Some of you dads are thinking, *Look, I'm just not a touchy, affectionate guy.* You're going to have to get over it and learn to touch. Your kids desperately need it. I'm not asking you to touch total strangers! I'm asking you to touch your kids.

Talk Personally

Real love requires you to know someone. You know someone when he shares personally. Dad, you need to reveal yourself to your children. How do you do this? By sharing, on a regular basis, your thoughts. Your values. Your hopes and dreams. Your victories and defeats. Your emotions.

You don't share everything. You don't share your secrets. These are for your wife and your best friend. But you need to share yourself with your children *every day*.

I recommend sharing one personal item per day per child. You can do this in the five to ten minute daily time I mentioned earlier. Say, "I had a hard day today," and tell the child what happened. Or, "Something neat happened today." "God answered my prayer." "I'm sad…I'm angry…I'm frustrated, I'm happy…"

By sharing personally, you're giving your child a window into your life. Every personal item you share is a gift of love. This kind of honest expression will automatically deepen your relationship.

Some of you dads are thinking, *Look, I'm just not very expressive.* I'll bet you're not. Most men aren't expressive by nature. Get over it. You need to work at this because your kids need to hear from your heart. Use your pad to jot down personal things you want to share with them. Sending cards or letters to your kids is a great way to express your love for them and what's going on in your life.

Transfer Your Spirituality

Dad, nothing is more important than transferring to your children your love for God and your commitment to Jesus Christ. This is your number one job as a dad (read Deuteronomy 6:5-7 again). My dad, Bill Clarke, always told my brother, Mark, and me, "Guys, the most important thing in life is walking with Jesus and growing in your relationship with Him. If you don't do that, your mother and I have failed as parents." I'm giving my kids the same message.

If you don't know God, you can't transfer your love for Him to your children. To know God, you have to know His Son, Jesus Christ.

> I am the way, and the truth, and the life; no one comes to the Father but through Me (John 14:6).

To know Jesus, you must accept the wonderful sacrifice He made for you more than two thousand years ago.

> For I delivered to you as of first importance what I also received, that Christ died for our sins according to the Scriptures, and that He was buried, and that He was raised on the third day according to the Scriptures (1 Corinthians 15:3-4).

You are a sinner, which means you have done wrong, bad things in your life. Even one sin prevents you from connecting to God, who is holy and righteous and perfect. The moment you believe that Jesus died for you, that He paid the price for your sins (death), and that He rose from the dead, you personally know God through Jesus.

Dad, once you know God, model for your children a Christian life that works. Practice daily devotions (and let your kids see you doing them), pray throughout the day, pray with your kids regularly, read your Bible, serve in the church, and be accountable to one other Christian man for your job as husband and father.

Find ways to teach spiritual principles to your kids. Communicate spiritual truths in one-on-one conversations and in a weekly family devotional time. Tell your kids how God is guiding and directing and teaching you. Use real-life situations to show them how the Bible applies to your life.

If you have the guts, ask your wife regularly how you're doing as a dad. She'll know because she misses nothing that affects her kids. If you have the guts, ask each of your kids regularly how you're doing as a dad. Don't assume you're doing a great job! Ask and keep on asking. And make the necessary changes.

Marriage Enrichment Steps

1. Caveman, what kind of dad did you have when you were growing up? What kind of relationship did he build with you? What did your dad do well? What did he do poorly?

2. What are your strengths as a dad? What are your weaknesses?

3. Right now, ask your wife how she feels you're doing as a dad. Ask her to tell you how you can improve.

4. Which of the four *Ts* (time, touch, talk personally, and transfer your spirituality) do you need to work on the most? Decide now what you'll do in the next month to improve, and ask your wife to hold you accountable on a weekly basis.

5. Ask your wife how she'll respond to you when you're doing a good job as a dad to your kids.

11

Cinderella, You're Allowing Mistreatment

Speak Up and Earn His Love

Remember how Cinderella endured all that terrible, cruel treatment from her mean stepmother and her worthless stepsisters? She slaved away all day, doing every menial and thankless task in the house. Her performance was never good enough, and she often had to do jobs over again. Her family constantly criticized and belittled her. No one cared about her needs.

Through it all, Cinderella kept her cheerful attitude and continued serving her nasty relatives with barely a word of complaint. She always believed that things would just work out someday and that the prince would carry her off to his castle.

This is a fairy tale, but I believe it has deeper meaning. Chances are very good that you are living out this story in your marriage. How so? you ask. This is how: You are allowing your husband to mistreat you, and you're doing nothing about it. You are today's version of Cinderella, continuing to be the best wife you can be in the face of poor treatment from your Caveman. You hope and pray for change, but you take no action to create that change.

The odds of your husband suddenly and miraculously treating you better are about as good as the odds of Cinderella getting the prince. I know she did get the prince, but hers is a completely fictional story. A fantasy! Unless you do something, your husband will continue to treat you with a lack of sensitivity, understanding, and love.

If you act like a doormat, you'll become a doormat.

What Is Mistreatment?

Here's my definition of mistreatment by a husband: Any violation of biblical instruction about his role as a husband. Here are six biblical roles your husband is to fulfill:

1. to love you as Christ loved the church (Ephesians 5:25)
2. to lead you in every area (Ephesians 5:23-24) as a Christlike servant (Matthew 20:28; John 13:3-5)
3. to treat you softly, gently, and with tender care (1 Peter 3:7)
4. to be a godly man (Matthew 22:36-37)
5. to energetically pursue you in romance (Song of Solomon)
6. to constantly build you up with compliments and encouraging words (Song of Solomon)

If he fails to treat you as these verses instruct him, he is mistreating you. I know these standards are high, but they describe the way God wants him to act toward you.

More specifically, husbands mistreat their wives in two ways.

Verbal mistreatment includes criticism that is not constructive, but offensive. Personal attacks on your character, behavior, or appearance. Sarcasm. Belittling, demeaning comments. Raising his voice to you in anger. Swearing. Name-calling. Mocking. Mentioning divorce.

Behavioral mistreatment includes ignoring you, sharing his view and not listening to yours, and throwing things or doing property damage. Failing again and again to do chores. Making promises and breaking them. Making decisions without you. Lack of romance. Refusing to have sex with you. Refusing to help with the kids. Controlling behavior. Selfish behavior.

The bottom line is this: If you feel mistreated by your Caveman, he has almost certainly mistreated you. In other words, you define mistreatment—he doesn't. If you feel angry and hurt by something he says or does, he has mistreated you.

Here's one exception: You may have somehow misunderstood or misinterpreted something he said or did. Even in a case like this, you still need to bring up the issue and talk it through.

Good Husbands Mistreat

I'm not referring to husbands who are bona fide, abusive dirtballs. This chapter is not designed to help you deal with a husband who is involved in some form of serious, out-of-control sin, such as an affair, physical violence, sexual addiction, drug or alcohol addiction, gambling, refusing to work for a living, or vicious verbal attacks. If your husband is sinning in one of these areas, you'll need to mount a dramatic, aggressive, tough-love campaign. Get my book *I Don't Love You Anymore*.

I'm writing about good, decent, Christian husbands who are mistreating their wives. This kind of insensitivity is still very serious and does damage to you, to him, to the kids, and to your marriage. My experience indicates that it is happening in many Christian marriages.

Stop the Cinderella Thinking

Your insensitive Caveman husband is mistreating you, and you're doing zero about it. He's not a bad guy. In fact, he's a good guy, and he does love you. But mistreatment is still mistreatment, and his behavior is limiting your marital intimacy. You put up with mistreatment because you believe one of two Cinderella thinking mistakes.

First, you may believe that if you just keep on faithfully loving him and meeting his needs, he'll eventually stop hurting you and treat you with more sensitivity and love. Wrong. He doesn't even realize he's mistreating you. If you don't tell him, he'll never know. He sees you acting content as if you are and he watches you do all the usual things for him, so he figures everything in the marriage is fine. The fact that he's limiting your intimacy won't dawn on him. Remember, he's a Caveman.

By the way, how is your "change him with love and kindness" approach working? You've been at it now for a number of years. Yeah, I thought so. Not changing, is he?

You may be wondering if this agrees with 1 Peter 3:1-2: "In the same way, you wives, be submissive to your own husbands so that even if any of them are disobedient to the word, they may be won without a word by the behavior of their wives, as they observe your chaste and respectful behavior."

These verses teach submission, not subservience or passivity. The wife is always to model purity and excellent behavior, but she is also to follow the verses that instruct her to speak up in a loving and firm way. The Proverbs 31 wife was submissive, but she was also very assertive and active, and her husband respected her.

Also, other passages teach that we should confront sin (Matthew 18:15-17) and speak the truth (Ephesians 4:15; Colossians 3:9). The bottom line is this: When you look at the whole of Scripture, you see God instructing wives to model submission and excellent behavior *and* to be assertive and worthy of respect.

Second, you may believe that your man isn't that bad and that you'll be okay if he doesn't change. *Hey,* you say to yourself at least a hundred times a week, *he's a good man. He works hard at his job. He goes to church. He doesn't beat me, drink like a fish, or sleep around. He could be a lot worse. I have to accept the fact that he won't change. I can live with that.*

You've given up hope of ever having a deeper, more intimate bond with your Caveman. His insensitive words and behavior do hurt, but you think they can't be helped. You just paint on your brave smile and ride the Cinderella coach on that long, lonely road to the horizon.

Some older wives in your church family or social circle may have convinced you that the man you have is as good as he can be. They've persuaded you that men are "just that way," and you can do nothing about it. For good measure they may have thrown in the classic enabler line: "Honey, you just have to make Jesus your husband."

These two Cinderella ways of thinking are wrong. Wrong. Wrong. Wrong. If you believe your husband will change because of your excellent behavior as a wife, you're sadly mistaken. If you believe your husband can't change and you tolerate his mistreatment, you are in error. In both cases, *you* are part of the problem. You are enabling him to stay exactly the kind of husband he is now. He's convinced you're okay with who he is, so he has absolutely zero motivation to do anything differently.

If you've been guilty of one of these Cinderella mistakes, it's time to get rid of your evening gown and glass slippers. Stop being so nice and forgiving and fake all the time. Start being honest with yourself and with him.

The Dialogue

Cinderella: "I'm just a nice person. I can't help but be nice to him."

Me: "No, you're not nice. You aren't telling him the truth, as you're instructed to do in Ephesians 4:25, Colossians 3:9, and many other places in Scripture. That's not nice. And you aren't giving your husband a chance to change. That's not nice either. You're also allowing your children to learn that it's okay to mistreat a woman. That too is not nice. You aren't nice, you're codependent."

Cinderella: "But I have to submit to him, don't I?"

Me: "No, not when he's sinning. You don't submit to sin. Rather, you confront it every time" (Matthew 5:23-24; 18:15-17).

Cinderella: "I don't get angry with my husband. It's not ladylike or Christlike."

Me: "First, you *are* angry deep down. Second, it's okay and healthy to be angry. We're actually commanded to express it the same day we feel it (Ephesians 4:26-27). Third, Christ was angry and for good reason (Matthew 21:12-13; Mark 8:32-33). You have good reason to be angry too."

Cinderella: "He always says he's sorry after doing or saying something that hurts me."

Me: "Sorry isn't good enough. True repentance includes being sorry but focuses on change. If you're okay with him just being sorry, that's all he's going to give you."

Cinderella: "Most of the time he's blunt and abrasive because he's had a hard, stressful day at work."

Me: "So? That's no excuse. Sinful behavior is sinful behavior. Treating you roughly is not an acceptable or effective way to handle his stress. Speaking of stress, his behavior is stressing you, isn't it?"

Cinderella: "I saw my mom take mistreatment from my dad for years. I guess that's where I learned to put up with it. I think it's normal. My ex-husband also treated me with insensitivity too much of the time."

Me: "You mom was your codependent Yoda. She taught you to tolerate mistreatment, but you can change that pattern and stop the generational sin. We'll work in therapy on your past pain, and that will help you be more assertive with your husband."

Cinderella: "I'm afraid to stand up to him. Will he get really angry and be out of control? Will he put up a fight and battle me? Will my changed behavior disrupt the kids' lives? Will he leave me or maybe even divorce me? Will I find out he doesn't love me enough to change?"

Me: "These are valid fears. When you start standing up to him, you may be in for a battle. He's used to mistreating you and getting away with it. He won't like getting static from you. You have to decide that following the Bible and finding your assertive, Christlike voice is best for everyone in the family. If you want to be treated well and build a close marriage, you must demand good treatment. If he's truly a good Christian man, he will change in response to your changes."

Your Five-Step Assertiveness Program

I've led many wives through these five steps of assertiveness training. I've seen them work over and over again. Now it's your turn.

Sign Up a Support Person

You can't carry off this assertiveness program on your own. It's too tough. You need to find one married female Christian (not a family member) who is willing to provide frequent encouragement and accountability. She could be a close friend or a mentor, such as a leader in your church or a pastor's wife.

You'll tell her everything about your husband's mistreatment and how you've tolerated it. You'll ask her to keep you on the assertiveness track by praying with you, asking you to share how you're being assertive, giving you pep talks when needed, calling you a wimp when you falter, and gently but firmly getting you back in the saddle.

Meet with her once a week and stay in touch by phone. Call her when you need to vent or get some encouragement. The Bible teaches us to "bear one another's burdens" (Galatians 6:2), and that's exactly what your support person is doing.

Keep a Mistreatment Journal

Buy a small pad and record every instance of his mistreatment.

Use three columns: one for what happened, one for your emotional reaction, and one for what you did about it. Do this for two weeks, and you'll get a pretty good baseline measurement of the mistreatment episodes. You may be surprised at how many or how few instances you record.

Your journal will help you track the frequency of mistreatment and the specific nature of it. When does it usually happen? Does it follow a recognizable pattern? What forms does it take? How long does it last? What exact words and behaviors does he exhibit?

The journal will help you understand the mistreatment and your reaction to it. What emotions do you have when it happens? What fearful thoughts come into your mind? What do you usually do in response?

Initially, of course, you will not be jotting down any impressive, assertive responses. You'll jot down your usual, wimpy responses. As you improve, you'll be able to write down more healthy, assertive behaviors. This will motivate and encourage you.

Share your journal with your support person. Going over it with her (and your therapist, if you have one) will greatly enhance the learning process. If your husband wants to know what you're using the journal for, tell him. It's no secret. Tell him it's a tool to help you be more honest and assertive with him when he mistreats you. If he's willing and has a good attitude, the two of you can go over the journal together. It can also help *him* correct his insensitive behavior.

One-Way Every Time

Using the one-way communication technique I explained in chapter 6, tell him *every time* he mistreats you. That's right, every time. A breach of respect has occurred and caused some damage, and your job is to let him know as soon as possible. Tell him the truth in a loving way (Ephesians 4:15). Be brief. Just a few sentences will get the job done.

If you can't verbally point out his mistake immediately, at least do it by the end of the day. As Ephesians 4:26-27 commands, you need to clean out difficult, painful emotions each day. You could use part of a regularly scheduled couple talk time to lay it on him.

Tell him your emotions and what he did, and ask him (when he's ready) to apologize and talk the situation out. Then walk away or be silent.

> Honey, I have something difficult to say to you. I was angry and hurt by your sarcastic comment this morning about my cooking ability. I felt insulted. When you're ready, I'd like to hear an apology and discuss what happened.

If you stuff your emotions and say nothing, a lot of bad things happen: You may stuff and stuff and stuff and then periodically blow up in anger. You may get depressed. You will be bitter and resentful. His behavior will never change. Worst of all, you run the risk of hitting the wall one day and leaving the marriage because all your love is gone.

Tell Him Why You Think He Mistreated You

Your Caveman has zero insight into why he mistreats you. He probably doesn't even realize he's doing it at all. Pointing out his mistreatment in the one-way manner is good, but it's not good enough. On his own, he still won't try to figure out why he acts in insensitive, hurtful ways. Seeking an explanation for his poor relationship skills would mean digging into personal matters, and he's spent his whole life staying away from that sensitive area.

Your job is to use well-placed, one-way observations to show him the reasons why you think he mistreats you. He has a relationship disability. An integral part of the rehabilitation process is having a coach who will show him exactly where it comes from. You are that coach. He's not asking for your help, but you're going to give it to him anyway. The insights you share can play a big part in his change process. You won't give him this kind of insight every time because you won't always have an opinion about the reason. But when you do have a good guess, tell him.

Wife: "That temper outburst last night reminded me of your dad. You look and act just like him when you lose it. Until you deal with him and your feelings about how he raised you, you'll keep on raging and hurting me and the kids."

Wife: "When I said no to sex this morning, you shut me out and ignored me for three hours. You still haven't healed from your ex-wife rejecting you, sexually and in other ways. So when you feel like I've rejected you, you close down and won't talk about it. When you're ready, I want you to talk to me about what she did to you. When that pain is out of you, you'll be able to open up to me and receive all my love."

Wife: "You're stuffing your work stress again tonight. You've got the television on, and you've been avoiding me for the past two hours. I'm hurt and frustrated. If you'd share the work problems with me, you'd be happier, and we'd be closer. But that's up to you."

Wife: "The past month, you've pulled back from me. You're preoccupied with your work and sports. You don't seem too happy with me or your life. I think one of the reasons is that you've drifted from the Lord. You're not having regular quiet times, and you've missed church several Sundays. I'm hurt that you're shutting me out, and I'm also concerned about you. If you want to talk about what's going on and want my help to get back on track spiritually, find me and we'll talk."

Wife: "Did you notice what you just did? Our conversation was starting to get a little personal, so you made a joke to lighten the mood. That's something you do a lot. It ticks me off because I need closeness with you. I've seen your dad and brother do the same joke thing to avoid personal subjects. I'd like to talk about this and what we can do about it. When you're ready, let me know, and we'll schedule a talk time."

Give Him a Consequence

Most often, *individuals only change when they experience sufficient pain to motivate new behavior.* Being honest and direct verbally with him is important, but it won't be enough to motivate him to work on changing his insensitive ways. He must face some consequences for his mistreatment of you, or he won't feel the need to change.

Use the one-way technique and tell him you'll wait for his heartfelt apology and willingness to discuss the incident fully. You want to see him try to figure out why he mistreated you. During this waiting period, before he comes back to you, the marriage is temporarily suspended. You're still married, but not in the same, "everything's okay and normal" way. If everything seems fine, he has no reason to apologize and work at resolving the issue.

So everything must *not* be fine. You will be quiet, reserved, and pulled back from him. No real communication about any other topic, no affection, and no time together until he returns and is genuinely involved in talking out what happened.

No sex either until he's truly repentant. Repentant means being sorry, listening and reflecting back as you vent, and working to uncover why he mistreated you. I have a funny feeling the temporary suspension of sex may get his attention. You sometimes need to suspend marital sex (1 Corinthians 7:5), and this is one of those times. To engage in the intensely vulnerable and intimate act of intercourse before resolving a breach of respect (or at least before the process is begun) is very harmful to you, and you need to tell him that.

The Caveman way of resolving the problem is by having sex. That's not your way, and it won't work for you.

Cinderella, you will take a while to learn these assertiveness steps. Confronting his mistreatment won't be easy, but the benefits will be worth the effort: You will clean your system of anger and hurt and resentment, you will be able to forgive, you'll stay emotionally healthy, you'll give him repeated opportunities and motivation to change, you'll stay in love with him, and together you can build a more intimate bond.

Marriage Enrichment Steps

1. Ask your husband to tell you how he thinks he mistreats you. Ask him why he thinks he acts in these ways.

2. Being gentle but honest, tell your husband how he mistreats you—what he says and what he does. If you have any ideas why he makes these mistakes, share them with him.

3. Which of the two Cinderella thinking mistakes are you guilty of? Which of the reasons or excuses in the Dialogue section can you relate to? What are you afraid might happen if you speak up and show assertiveness with your husband?

4. Which of the five assertiveness steps are you willing to try at this time? Which one would be most effective for you?

5. Ask your husband what consequences would motivate him to change in this area.

6. Discuss how he can avoid consequences.

12

Caveman, You're Being Insensitive

Be Gentle and Earn Her Respect

Caveman insensitivity began back in the Garden of Eden when Adam, the first Caveman (so to speak), blamed Eve for the first sin. When God asked him if he had eaten from the forbidden tree, Adam responded, "The woman whom You gave to be with me, she gave me from the tree, and I ate" (Genesis 3:12).

Talk about your lame excuses! What a weasel! Instead of protecting his wife, he tried to pin the sin on her. Eve must have been thinking, *Thanks a lot, Adam. Your support makes me feel so special.*

Adam was the first insensitive Caveman, but he certainly wasn't the last. A Caveman, by nature, has an insensitive streak a mile wide. He tends to be selfish, crude, dense, rough around the conversational edges, controlling, sarcastic, flippant, blunt, forgetful, and devoid of any ability to understand a woman.

Hey, I have a great idea! Let's put this incredibly insensitive Caveman into a relationship with an unbelievably sensitive Cinderella. Yeah, and let's have them get married and live together. What could go wrong? Actually, just about everything.

Do you think Cinderella, with her built-in hair-trigger sensitivity, will get angry and hurt by her bull-in-the-china-shop Caveman? You'd better believe it. This dramatic difference in sensitivity is a major problem in marriage.

It Doesn't Take Much

Caveman, it doesn't take much to upset your Cinderella. She's emotional, moody, and easily offended. She watches you like a hawk and misses nothing. She scrutinizes everything you say and do and runs it through her sensitivity grid. Something you consider trivial and inconsequential is very likely to feel like a personal attack to her. A word, a glance, a sigh, or a certain tone of voice can cause an intense reaction of pain in her. She may not tell you, but inside she's hurt and feeling unloved and mistreated.

Here's one small example of how difficult dealing with a sensitive wife can be. Out of nowhere, she says to you, "I'm getting fat." That comment is shocking enough, but she's also looking at you intently and expecting a response. This is a classic no-win situation for you, the hapless Caveman. Regardless of what you say, you will be insensitive and wrong and offensive.

You say, "No, you're not fat." She says, "I *am* fat! I just told you I was fat! I think I know what fat is. Check out these thighs. Would you call them thin?"

Or, you say nothing. That doesn't work either. She says, "Didn't you hear me? I said I was fat! What we have here is a fat wife who is being ignored by her husband. I know you think I'm overweight and unattractive. That's why you're not saying anything."

You say, "Well, honey, I guess you have gained a few pounds. So have I. No big deal." Now, you're dead meat, even though you have told the truth. "I knew it! I knew you thought I was fat! How long have you thought I was fat?" Good luck answering that last question without offending her.

Treat Her Like a Queen

Caveman, the "I'm getting fat" scenario is just one tiny example of the challenge you face in living with a hypersensitive Cinderella.

Learning to be sensitive and understanding is difficult, but you can do it. Scripture makes it clear that you must treat her like a queen.

Jesus loved women and treated them with dignity and respect. To Him, they were equal in value to men. This was revolutionary thinking for His culture. Jesus shocked the Jewish world by being the first rabbi to allow women to be His disciples. He invited Mary, Martha, and Mary Magdalene (she might have been a former prostitute!) into His inner circle. Jesus is our example, men.

The key verse on how to treat a wife is 1 Peter 3:7. Read this verse very carefully, Caveman, because it packs quite a punch:

> You husbands in the same way, live with your wives in an understanding way, as with someone weaker, since she is a woman; and show her honor as a fellow heir of the grace of life, so that your prayers will not be hindered.

God commands you to treat your wife as a precious, priceless person. You are to treat her better than anyone else on earth. She is your equal and deserves dignity and respect. You are to handle her gently, kindly, and softly. You are to adore and cherish her. You are to express the utmost tenderness for her.

If you fail to treat her with this kind of understanding and sensitivity, your selfishness will block your access to God! That's the worst possible consequence, and that's how important this is to God. Treat her well, or your spiritual life will suffer. One of the main reasons so many husbands are spiritually dry is that they mistreat their wives—whether they mean to or not.

The Checklist of Insensitivity

I've compiled a list of many common insensitive Caveman behaviors. It's not exhaustive by any means, but it will help you get a good idea of how insensitive you are and where you need to improve. Check the ones you feel apply to you. If you're not sure, ask your wife. She'll know.

Verbal Mistreatment
Mr. Logic

- "You don't know what you're talking about."
- "You're not making any sense."
- "You're too emotional."
- "Here's what I'd do in the situation if I were you."
- "That's life, honey."
- "Let it go, it's in the past."
- Interrupting her and telling her she's wrong to feel or think a certain way.
- Telling her how to feel or think.
- Playing devil's advocate and defending the person who has hurt or angered her.

The Wonderful World of Sarcasm

- "Oh, you're perfect, I guess."
- "It has to be your way, doesn't it?"
- "Who died and made you queen?"
- "Oh, sure, that'll work."

Avoiding Intimate Conversations

- Refusing to talk.
- Ignoring her when she's talking about something you don't want to talk about.
- Being cynical.
- Cracking a joke to lighten the mood and prevent the conversation from getting too deep.

Poor Conflict-Resolution Skills

- Raising your voice.
- Refusing to listen to her side of the argument.
- Leaving and not coming back to restart the conversation.

- Making personal attacks.
- Laughing at her feelings and opinion.
- Lying to her to avoid conflict.

Criticism

Throwing barbs about her cooking, her housecleaning, her parenting, her spending, her weight or appearance, her family, or her intelligence.

Behavioral Mistreatment

- Controlling the remote.
- Being lazy and not doing your share of the chores.
- Promising and not delivering.
- Forgetting to do chores.
- Forgetting special days like her birthday, your anniversary, Valentine's Day, and Mother's Day.
- Remembering special days but not doing much for her.
- Doing your own fun activities and leaving her with the kids.
- Working too many hours and not telling her when you'll be home.
- Refusing to do activities she enjoys doing.
- Controlling the money.
- Giving her a monthly allowance.
- Making financial decisions without consulting her.
- Making other significant decisions without consulting her.
- Driving like a maniac.
- Refusing to spend time with her relatives.
- Pressuring her or forcing her to have sex without the proper emotional and spiritual preparation.
- Not changing the toilet paper roll.
- Not lifting or lowering the toilet seat.

- Not cleaning your whiskers from the sink after you shave.
- Belching and not saying "excuse me."
- Making other sounds and not saying "excuse me."

Do any of these verbal and behavioral examples of mistreatment look familiar? I certainly could check off quite a few. Be man enough to admit your mistakes and work on correcting them.

The Dialogue

Caveman: "I don't mean to hurt her with what I say and do."

Me: "You are hurting her whether you mean to or not."

Caveman: "She's too sensitive."

Me: "No, she's a woman. They're all sensitive. You are too insensitive."

Caveman: "I can't listen to her when she's venting about something I've said or done wrong. She takes way too long."

Me: "She needs to vent, and she'll rehearse what happened until she knows you understand. Listen, reflect, and have a good attitude, and you can shorten the time of suffering. If you resist, you'd better get comfortable."

Caveman: "I don't want to become some overly sensitive wimp of a man. I'm a man's man."

Me: "A real man learns to be sensitive to his wife. Jesus was the ultimate man, and He was sensitive to women. Of course, you can stay a macho man and have a miserable wife and a mediocre marriage. It's up to you."

Caveman: "I can't be perfect!"

Me: "Nobody's asking you to be perfect. With

God's help and your hard work, you will improve dramatically. She can live with a certain amount of insensitivity as long as you're being sensitive most of the time."

Your Five-Step Sensitivity Program

In the previous chapter, I took your dear Cinderella through five steps of assertiveness training. Now it's time for you to learn how to be sensitive.

Sign Up a Support Person

Just as your wife needs someone to come alongside her in her assertiveness program, you also need a support person. Don't play Lone Ranger. You'll never make it. Read the Support Person section in chapter 11 and follow those same guidelines: Contract with a married Christian man, tell him all about your insensitivity, ask him to hold you accountable, pray with him, meet once a week, and stay in touch by phone. If he's open to it, you can hold him accountable in his areas of insensitivity.

Keep a Mistreatment Journal

Read the Mistreatment Journal section of chapter 11 and follow the steps I outline there. Buy a pad and note every time you mistreat your wife. Use three columns: one for what you did or said, one for your emotional reaction, and one for what you did after the incident (such as walked away, apologized, or acted as though it never happened).

Keep the journal for two weeks. You'll learn how often you mistreat your wife and exactly how you do it. You may be able to identify what triggers you to act in these insensitive ways, such as stress, fatigue, feeling controlled, wanting to maintain control, or spiritual apathy. Your wife will be keeping her journal at the same time. Every few days, or at least once a week, sit down with her to compare journals. Finding out how each of you view the episodes of mistreatment will be interesting and instructive.

Urge Her to Catch You

Give your wife permission to catch you every time you are being insensitive. This is good for her assertiveness and good for your recognition of the problem. You don't even realize you're being insensitive, so you need her to point it out. Eventually, you'll be able to catch yourself and eliminate many of the insensitive episodes.

Provide her with a code phrase (Cinderellas love codes, remember?) to use to alert you to your insensitivity: "I think you're being insensitive." "I believe you've crossed the line." "Time out." "You just cost yourself sex tonight, buddy." Just kidding about that last one.

When you hear the code phrase, don't fight it or resist in any way. Believe your wife because she is the only one who is able to say when you're being insensitive. If she says you are, you are. Period. As soon as you hear the code phrase, do four things: Take a quick break to simmer down and chill out (saying a brief prayer would be a good idea), come back to her and apologize, pursue her if she's pulled away, and talk the situation out.

Say You're Sorry, Pursue Her, and Talk It Out

Your run-of-the-mill Caveman doesn't apologize well. He hates to show weakness and to admit that he's wrong. In fact, he often thinks he didn't do anything wrong. Believe me, Caveman, if your Cinderella is upset, chances are very good that you've done something wrong.

First, here's how not to apologize. Don't say, "I'm sorry if I offended, hurt, or angered you." What do you mean, *if?* There's no if about it. Something you did or said actually happened, and it bothered her. Don't say, "I'm sorry, but…" But what? The *but* cancels out the sorry part, and she doesn't want to hear your lame excuse.

Don't say, "You misunderstood me." Now, you're blaming her rather than accepting responsibility. Don't say, "We." "We" indicates that she is at fault too. That won't make her happy. Don't say, "I'm sorry" in a resentful or exasperated way. If you can't say it in a heartfelt way, wait until you can. But do say you're sorry. Acting as though nothing happened further insults and hurts your wife.

If you said "I'm sorry" in the wrong way, you caused additional hurt, and now you must say another "I'm sorry" for your lame apology and still repeat your "I'm sorry" in the right way for your original insensitive offense.

An effective apology includes three critical steps. First say the initial "I'm sorry" in a heartfelt and genuine way right to her face. Use words like these: "Honey, I'm sorry. I blew it. I was wrong, and I upset you. Please forgive me. Let's talk it out when you're ready."

Second, if she gets emotional and goes silent or walks away, you must go after her. She wants you to pursue her. She wants and needs you to come to her, talk out the incident, reassure her of your love, and win her back. If she's not ready to talk, leave for a few minutes and then come back. Keep coming back until she's ready to talk about what happened.

Third, be prepared for several talks with her about the insensitive mistake you made. She'll do all the talking and venting initially. Listen, reflect back to her what you're hearing, and continue to say, "I'm sorry." One "I'm sorry," even if heartfelt, is never enough for a woman. Keep saying it until she believes it.

When she has finished venting, she needs to hear from you. Without making any excuses, tell her why you think you acted in such an insensitive way. Do your best to figure out what triggered your words or behavior. If you can't think of any explanation at the time, jot down the incident on your pad and tell her you'll study it and get back to her.

Watch Your Mouth

As a Caveman—especially an angry or frustrated Caveman—you have a bad habit of being too harsh and abrasive when you speak to your Cinderella. This kind of insensitivity crushes her and does real damage to her self-esteem and her respect for you.

Remember three verses when you speak to your wife. First, 1 Peter 3:7 says to be gentle. Second, Proverbs 16:24 says pleasant words are sweet and healing. Third, 1 Corinthians 13:5 says love "does not act unbecomingly."

Keep your tone within reasonable limits. Avoid sarcasm and yelling. Don't use vulgar (or worse) language of any kind. Stay away from the words *never, always,* and *should*. Refrain from any critical personal attacks. Don't roll your eyes. Don't sigh loudly.

Communication is a self-correcting process. If you make a mistake as you're speaking—whether she catches you or you catch yourself—stop the conversation immediately and take a break. Come back, apologize for your mistake, and continue the conversation. I'll go into much more detail about conflict resolution in a later chapter.

Marriage Enrichment Steps

1. Caveman, how did your dad treat your mom? What kind of insensitive behavior did he model in his treatment of your mom? How did your mom react to his insensitivity?

2. Using the checklist of insensitivity, tell your wife the specific insensitive words and behaviors you are guilty of the most. Suck up your courage and ask her to tell you the most common ways you are insensitive to her.

3. Who can you ask to be your support person?

4. Which of the five steps in the sensitivity program are you willing to take? Which steps would help you the most? Ask your wife which steps she'd like you to take.

5. How are you in the apology department? Which of the "I'm sorry" mistakes do you make most often?

13

Cinderella, You're Not Being Sexy

Be Interested, Be Aggressive, and Be Responsive

Cinderella, you'd better sit down and get a firm grip on the armrest. I'm going to take you where very few women have gone: into the strange, twisted, and wonderful world of your Caveman's sexuality. I hope you haven't just had a meal. If you have, better keep a bucket handy. Here we go.

The Caveman's Priorities

Your Caveman loves sex. He thinks about it constantly. You could say he's obsessed with it. In fact, go ahead and say that because it's true. Sex is his number one human need in life.

When women list their priorities from most important to least important, here are the typical results:

1. children	6.	health
2. family	7.	job
3. friends	8.	finances
4. home	9.	sex
5. church		

As you can see, sex is well down the list. It barely makes the list.

When men rank their priorities, here's what they come up with:

1. sex
2. sex
3. sex
4. sex
5. sex
6. sex
7. sex
8. sex
9. food

Believe me, I'm not kidding. Ask your Caveman if you doubt me.

Rats and Sex

Laboratory studies with rats confirm the amazing power of sex in the life of males. A male rat is placed in a cage. One corner of the cage has a lever. The lever is connected to electrodes in the sexual pleasure center of his rat brain. When the male rat hits this lever, he receives a jolt of sexual pleasure.

You'll never guess what the male rat does after he receives that first rat orgasm from hitting the lever. He hits that lever over and over and over again. He doesn't eat, he doesn't drink, and he doesn't sleep. He just keeps hitting the lever until he dies from sheer exhaustion and malnutrition. Researchers tell us that he dies with a smile on his face.

What does the female rat do after she hits the lever and receives her first jolt of sexual pleasure? Well, she doesn't seem to be that impressed. She largely ignores the lever and spends most of her time tidying up the cage and caring for her baby rats. Every now and then, when she has nothing better to do, she'll waltz over and hit the lever.

Sex and Memory

As a woman, you have a phenomenal memory. You can remember what you were wearing at your third-grade piano recital. Your husband can't remember what he had for lunch today. But the one glaring exception in your incredible memory bank is your recall of sexual activity. Your Caveman, however, can remember everything about your sexual life as a couple.

You are consistently incorrect when you try to remember the last time you had sex with him. You almost always think it was "just a few days ago." You are wrong. Your Caveman can remember the exact date and time of day and what you were wearing.

You also seem to conveniently forget planned sexual encounters. During a talk the two of you had on Monday evening, he asked for sex on Wednesday evening. You will remember everything he said except the plan for sex. He will forget everything you said except the plan for sex.

Give That Man an Award!

You think your Caveman is always chasing you for sex. Well, he is. For him, three or four days without sex seems like an eternity. In Cinderella time, it's just three or four days. In Caveman time, it's like two or three years.

But let me tell you something that will surprise you. You have no idea how many times your Caveman does not pursue you for sex when he wants to. You're tired, the kids are around, it's too late, or you're busy with a project. And so your courageous Caveman bites the bullet and forces his sexual urges to the side.

He walks down the hallway, a lonely and terribly frustrated Caveman. He deserves an award, some kind of plaque suitable for framing, for all the times he graciously forgoes sex.

Your Caveman Needs Sex

Okay, forget the award idea. But understanding your Caveman's God-given need for sex is very important. Sex is like air to him. It's a big part of what makes him a man.

When he has sex with you regularly, he's confident. He feels loved by you. He feels close to you. He is at peace. He's happy. He feels like a man.

When he doesn't have sex with you regularly, just the opposite is true. He loses confidence. He feels rejected by you. He's irritable, edgy, moody, and unhappy. He feels angry and frustrated. He feels like less of a man.

I've used a lot of humor to make this point, but it's a very serious point, and you must get this: Your Caveman has a deep, vital need for regular sex with you.

The Bible and Sex

God makes it clear that sex is to be a healthy, regular part of a marriage relationship.

> The wife does not have authority over her own body, but the husband does; and likewise also the husband does not have authority over his own body, but the wife does. Stop depriving one another, except by agreement for a time, so that you may devote yourselves to prayer, and come together again so that Satan will not tempt you because of your lack of self-control (1 Corinthians 7:4-5).

Regular intercourse is not optional. It is essential to the ongoing development of intimacy in a marriage. If you deprive, defraud, and rob each other, Satan will take full advantage, and bad things will happen.

Intercourse is what gives you the "one flesh" experience (Genesis 2:24). When the two of you come together in intercourse, you are truly and completely one—spiritually, emotionally, and physically.

Cinderella, read the Song of Solomon and carefully study the Shulammite woman. She is a great example of what every man longs for in his woman. She was a shameless flirt with Solomon. She was unashamedly sensuous. She was thrilled with Solomon's body and complimented him on his various physical parts (Song of Solomon 5:10-16). She was somewhat self-conscious about her appearance (Song of Solomon 1:6), but that didn't stop her from desiring Solomon and asking him to pursue her sexually (Song of Solomon 1:2-4; 3:1-4; 7:10-13).

The clear message in all these passages, particularly in the Song of Solomon, is that both the husband and the wife are to enjoy sex. Sex is not a service you perform for him! It is for you too! It is a deeper, more intense need for him, but God also made you to need it.

For you, as with many wives, sex may be a difficult part of marriage.

You will probably have to learn to experience sex as God designed it to be: pleasurable, fun, playful, stress-reducing, a wonderful escape, and a deep expression of intimacy. Men, though they can certainly have sexual hang-ups, usually are more naturally inclined to experience sex in those ways.

Let's look at some of the obstacles preventing you from letting yourself go and enjoying God's gift of sex with your husband.

The Dialogue

Cinderella: "I'm not that interested in sex because he doesn't prepare me for it. We don't talk that much, we don't pray together, and he's not known for his romance. I need to be emotionally and spiritually connected to him before I can give myself to him physically. And I need more help with the chores so I'm not exhausted by the end of the day."

Me: "You know what? You've hit the nail on the head. These are all valid reasons for you to not be that into sex. You need to sit him down and gently but firmly lay these concerns on him. If he wants an energetic and responsive woman in bed, he needs to improve in these areas of preparation. Reading this book together and applying the principles will certainly make a big difference."

Cinderella: "I think I just go through the motions sexually because of all my resentments against him. He's a good guy, but over the years he has hurt and disappointed me many times. I've held in my anger, and that's keeping me from opening up to him sexually. I give him sex, but it's like a chore."

Me: "Sit him down and tell him what you just

told me. Take a week and write him a letter describing all the times he hurt you in the past. Ask God to help you remember all the resentments you need to include. The purpose of the letter is to release your pain in an honest, direct way and to forgive him. Sit down with him, pray that God will use the letter to bring about forgiveness, and read it to him. Ask your husband to listen, reflect back to you what he hears you saying, and try to feel your pain. Take several weeks and have a number of talks in which you verbally vent about the letter's contents to him. If he can reflect and understand, healing and forgiveness will happen."

Cinderella: "I've got personal baggage from my past that stops me from enjoying sex."

Me: "Past personal pain often causes sexual blocks. Guilt over premarital sex, abuse as a child, rape, an abortion, a poor relationship with Dad, unresolved issues with an ex-spouse, and other painful experiences need to be faced so healing can occur. Tell your husband what your past pain is, and go with him to a Christian therapist to work it through. Do it together."

Cinderella: "The truth is, my husband is the one who resists sex. I want sex and have to chase him and pressure him to get it."

Me: "About twenty-five percent of husbands fall into this category. If you're doing all you can to be sexy and show interest, and he's not responding, then he's the one with the sexual problem. It could be anything, including unresolved past pain, resentments against you, too much stress, age, fatigue, and lack of confidence in his ability to perform. Sit him down and share your concerns. Ask him to tell you, when he's ready, what is blocking him. Use one-way communication to express your feelings each time he resists you sexually. If he won't talk it through with you, urge him to go to a Christian therapist with you. If he refuses to work on this problem, continue one-way communication as needed and pull back from him emotionally and physically. Seeing that he's losing you may motivate him to get help."

How to Prepare for Great Sex

Great sex is all about preparation. No couple can just spontaneously jump into bed and engage in passionate, meaningful, "one flesh" sex. Cinderella, here are six progressive steps that will prepare you (and your Caveman) for healthy sex.

Schedule Sex

Every weekend, on a Saturday or Sunday, sit down with your Caveman and schedule your sexual times for the upcoming week. This kind of planning has many benefits:

- You'll make sure sex happens even when life is busy.
- Your husband won't be in excruciating limbo, wondering when he can have sex.
- He won't need to pressure you.
- You won't have to put up with his usual crude and rather clumsy way of asking for sex.
- Both of you will be able to prepare for these special sexual periods.

Release Your Stress

When a man is stressed, he sees sex as a way to escape it and release it. When a woman is stressed, she sees sex as just one more stressful event. Cinderella, you must find healthy ways to vent and release your stress before you'll be ready to have sex.

Talk out your daily stress with friends. Talk it out with God in prayer. Talk it out with your husband. Try releasing your stress by writing in a journal. Read the Bible and meditate on God's Word to relieve stress. Try some basic relaxation exercises, such as tensing and relaxing your muscles from your toes up to your head.

Exercise Regularly

If you expect to keep your physical intimacy intact, you (and your Caveman) have to stay in shape. We peak physically at 18 years of age! After that, it's a long slide down the cliff. Unless you establish a regular program of exercise, you'll end up a flabby, pitiful couch potato. You are undoubtedly over 18, so let's get to work.

You need to exercise to be as attractive as possible to your mate. Do the best with the body you have. Also, exercise is the only way to fight fatigue. I see so many couples in their twenties, thirties, and forties—young couples in their prime years—who tell me, "Oh, Dr. Clarke, we'd like to have sex, but we're just too tired at the end of the day." I reply, "Really? Too tired, are we? What kind of regular exercise program does each of you follow?" I'm usually met with complete silence!

You must have energy to be physically intimate and to be emotionally intimate. Talking takes energy too. If I didn't exercise, I couldn't possibly listen to Sandy and be a good conversationalist. You think I like riding the stationary bike three days a week for 20 minutes at a crack? I hate it! I hate that bike. I say nasty things to it when I pass by it in the mornings. I like getting off that bike. Then I go looking for Sandy. She's usually hiding somewhere in the house. It's a little game we play.

Teamwork on Chores

Tell your husband that if he wants a responsive sexual partner, he needs to hold up his end of the household chores and kid jobs. If he fails to come through, he'll be making love to someone who's asleep, or at least exhausted and resentful.

Touching, Talking, and Praying

These three areas are essential in preparing for intercourse. You can do them during your couple conversation times four days a week and at other, more spontaneous times.

First, you need to have plenty of nonintercourse touching throughout the week: kissing, making out, fondling, and massaging. Many couples touch in significant ways only as part of foreplay. That's not enough touching. Touching without intercourse will keep you connected and physically close between your times of intercourse.

Talking and brief praying during your couple talk times will give you the emotional and spiritual connection you need to engage in successful intercourse. On the day of scheduled intercourse, make sure you talk and pray first. You'll be amazed at the difference this will make.

Be More Aggressive Sexually

Your Caveman opens the door to your home, and you're standing there wearing nothing but a skimpy negligee and a smile. You give him a big, wet kiss and say with a throaty, low voice, "My man is home and I know what he needs. I need the same thing. Badly. The kids are at a neighbor's house for a few hours. I thought we could, I don't know, play a card game or do the bills together. Ha. I'm kidding. I want your body. I've been waiting all day, and I can't wait any longer. I think you know the way to the bedroom, big boy. Stud. Take me, I'm yours."

This might be a little over the top, but I think you get the idea. You don't have to be some kind of a vamp, but please be more aggressive sexually. Show interest in him and his body. Pursue him sexually more of the time. Get your clothes off when you're having sex. Don't cover up! He thinks your body is beautiful, so let him see it.

Read in the Song of Solomon how the Shulammite woman came on to Solomon. She was one sexually aggressive lady! And she is your example. That's why her story is in the Bible.

More on sex later in the book. But these guidelines ought to get you started.

Marriage Enrichment Steps

1. Cinderella, ask your Caveman how often he thinks about having sex with you. Ask him what sex means to him as a man and as your husband.

2. Tell your husband how strong your sexual drive is. How often do you want to have sex with him? (All couples must come to a mutually satisfactory compromise regarding frequency and not leave this in limbo; one will accept fewer times than desired, and one will accept a few more times than desired.)

3. Tell him what is blocking you from desiring sex with him and being a responsive sexual partner. Is it lack of preparation, stuffed resentments, trauma, or other personal baggage? Talk about what you can do together to work through your obstacles.

4. If your husband is the one resisting sex, ask him to tell you why. Decide how you will work through his obstacles together.

5. What do you think of my six steps of preparation for sex? Which ones are you willing to apply this week?

14

Caveman, You're Not Being Romantic

Be a Modern-Day Solomon

Caveman, you are focused on sex and think about it all the time. I believe I made that point quite nicely in the previous chapter. You are usually kind, sweet, and loving in bed during the sexual experience. Unfortunately, your wife just goes through the motions and can't be sexually responsive. Have you noticed that? Do you wonder why she is less than thrilled with your sex life?

I'll tell you why. It's because you're as romantic as an old tennis shoe. Your Cinderella has a deep longing and need for *romance*. If she doesn't get romanced on a daily basis, she shuts down inside. She doesn't feel loved by you. She doesn't feel close to you. She literally cannot be an aroused, energetic lover.

Before and After the Wedding

Remember your dating days? Remember how sexy and passionate she was back then? Touching you. Kissing you. Making out with you. She couldn't keep her hands off you. Why was that? Because you were *romancing* her! Courting her! Charming her! Pursuing her! She responded to all your romantic words and actions with some serious emotional and physical love.

You got married and expected her vibrant, passionate love to continue. But it dried up all too quickly. Why? Because like millions of Cavemen before you, you stopped the romance! You stopped pursuing her romantically, so she stopped responding.

Read these classic Caveman after-the-wedding, nonromantic behaviors and see if you recognize yourself.

Hey, I Have an Erection!

The sum total of your romantic pursuit of your wife is getting an erection. When you notice your erection, you're ready for sex and think she should be too. Your erection is her signal that this is her lucky night.

Wouldn't it be great if your wife reacted by coming up real close to you and saying, "Hey, I couldn't help but notice your erection, so meet me in the bedroom in ten minutes."

Alas, that is not how it works. When she becomes aware of your arousal, she thinks, *Oh no, not again! I'm not ready for sex.* She needs more preparation than your erect male sex organ. It's enough for you but not for her.

I'm a Master of Asking for Sex

You have a very smooth, suave, and romantic way of asking your wife to come with you to the boudoir. "How about tonight?" "Do you think maybe…uh, you know, you and me?" "Hey, baby, got something for you." (Yes, it's a special gift.) "Let's have sex tonight." (That certainly cuts to the chase.) "Is your period over?" (Obviously, you're not really concerned about her physical well-being.) "Uhhh, uhhh, uhhh." (You grunt like a male gorilla.)

Sometimes you don't even make a sound. You come up behind her in the kitchen and grab her in that one certain way. In bed, you roll over and place your hand on her stomach. Or you snuggle up next to her and start fondling her.

Again, without any romantic buildup, these crude approaches are not well received. You sense resistance, don't you? Without any warning and without any expression of romantic love, she has no choice but to flinch and be apathetic at best. "Well, okay, if you have to have it." Is that the kind of reaction you want to keep on getting?

Just Me, My Wife, and the Television

You come home in the evening after work, and you're tired and stressed. You're glad to be home, and you just want to relax and unwind. After a nice dinner, you settle in to watch television. It helps you escape from life. You like to have your wife watch with you. You love her, of course, and you want to spend some time with her.

This is sad, but you consider this mutual television watching to be quality time. It gives you a warm, comfortable feeling. You feel close to your wife, and you're pretty sure she feels close to you. Ah, the good life.

The truth is, the two of you are close only in a geographical sense. Watching television together doesn't create the kind of romantic, intimate experience she longs to have with you. It works for you, but not for her.

Your Cinderella Needs Romance

Caveman, if you don't *regularly romance* your wife, she'll feel fat, ugly, unattractive, uninteresting, unhappy, and unloved. That's the brutal truth. If you don't believe me, ask her. She'll probably stay married to you, and I hope she does, but your marriage will be dry as dust.

Romance is the oil that keeps a love relationship running smoothly. What happens if you drain all the oil out of your car and try to drive it? The engine will seize up and die. Your lack of romance has caused your love relationship to seize up and die.

Well, that's the bad news. You stopped the romance, and your wife is cold, distant, not into sex, not warm and loving, irritable, and not too impressed with you. If things stay this way, it's going to be a long, hard trek to your golden anniversary.

The good news is that you can learn to be romantic again (or for the first time in your life) and bring the love and passion back into your woman and your marriage. And the intensity and depth you will experience will be better than you had back in your infatuation-fueled dating days.

Let me introduce you to two men who can help you in the romantic department.

The Original Mr. Romance

The first man is Solomon. He was perhaps the greatest lover who ever lived. The story of his love life with his sweetheart and eventual wife, the Shulammite woman, fills the Song of Solomon.

God had Solomon write this beautiful love poem so that a Caveman like you might get some critically important romantic clues. These guidelines worked thousands of years ago for Solomon, and they will work for you today.

Solomon was romantic during his courtship and throughout his entire marriage. He never stopped the romantic behaviors. He pursued the Shulammite woman and expressed romantic love for her in a variety of ways. I urge you to read the whole book with your beloved, but here are just a few snapshots of Solomon's romantic repertoire.

Kissing her. Some fantastic kissing happens in this book. They don't waste any time getting to each other's lips either. The second verse in the book is a kissing verse. And get this, Caveman: Song of Solomon 4:11 gives the clearest description you'll ever read of French kissing!

Touching and making out with her. Solomon and the Shulammite were real make-out artists. You'll find some very erotic touching and fondling going on in 2:6 and 8:3. PG-13, baby!

Complimenting her. Solomon compliments her throughout the book. He can't say enough nice things about her. In 4:1-7 and 7:1-9, he describes her body in loving detail. I mean, *whoa!* He calls the Shulammite "most beautiful of women" (1:8). What woman wouldn't just love to hear that—*often*—from her man?

Listening to her. Solomon had clearly mastered the skill of listening to his woman. He hung on her every word. In 2:14, he tells her he loves the sound of her voice.

How did the Shulammite respond to Solomon's romantic pursuit of her? With an undying, passionate love that boggles the mind. She received his love, basked in it, and gave it right back. She was crazy about him. Respected him. Praised him frequently. And best of all, Caveman, she couldn't get enough of his body. His romantic behaviors made him incredibly attractive to her (5:10-16). She was all over him!

The Dialogue

Caveman: "I'm just not a romantic guy."

Me: "Oh, okay. No problem. I guess you won't mind having zero passion and a boring, stale sex life."

Caveman: "She knows I love her. I don't have to be all romantic with her to prove my love."

Me: "Actually, she doesn't know you love her. Without romance, she can't feel loved. So you're wrong."

Caveman: "I can't afford to take her out to fancy restaurants and expensive shows."

Me: "Romance can be cheap. She doesn't need the big, extravagant outings to feel romanced. Those are great, but they don't happen often enough to create ongoing romance. The little, daily actions count the most."

Caveman: "My dad wasn't romantic, and he and Mom had a good, solid marriage."

Me: "I'll bet your mom wasn't too thrilled with his lack of romance. A good, solid marriage is a great blessing. But don't you want a great, passionate marriage with romance?"

Caveman: "My wife is just fine with how things are in our marriage. I don't think she needs any more romance."

Me:	"Baloney. She's probably given up on it. Ask her—and get ready for a shock."
Caveman:	"Doc, I'm blocking on being romantic. I have trouble when we get close, and I tend to resist emotional and physical intimacy."
Me:	"Let's work on the problem with you and your wife. It could be because of a number of factors: performance and confidence, stress and fatigue, and past unresolved pain from your family and other relationships."

Cliff Notes on Romance

Did you remember I mentioned that there were *two* guys who would help you become more romantic? Well, I'm the second guy. Here are some surefire ideas that will get some serious romance going in your marriage.

Real Kissing

Stop kissing your wife as if she's your sister. Or your aunt Mildred. Stop delivering those unbelievably short pecks. You might as well shake her hand. Are you afraid she'll give you some kind of disease?

She is your lover and needs to be kissed as though you mean it. She needs to know she's been kissed! Start giving her open-mouth, lubricated, sucky-face kisses that last eight to ten seconds. Give her more than one kiss too. One isn't enough to express your passionate love for your goddess, is it?

She's like Lauren Bacall in that classic Humphrey Bogart movie, *To Have and Have Not*. When Bogie kisses her, Lauren purrs, "I like that. I'd like more."

Every time you kiss her, you should also do two other romantic behaviors. First, hug her. Get your hands around her in a tender embrace. Brush back her hair and put your hands on her beautiful face. Second, after the hug and several kisses, tell her, "I love you,

_____." Use her real name, not "snookums" or "sweet cakes" or another one of your pet names for her.

Kiss her two or three times, hug her, and say "I love you" every chance you get: in the morning when you first awaken, when you're going off to work, when you arrive home after work, later in the evening on the couch during your couple talk time, and just before you go to bed.

Touching and Making Out

You need to be touching her in nonintercourse foreplay throughout the week. There are all kinds of terrific touching you can do without moving on to intercourse: kissing, fondling, massaging... You know, the kind of intense touching you did back before you got married. You're married now, so you don't have to feel any guilt. You can be on the couch or in bed. You can have your clothes on or off.

This kind of physical pleasuring will make her feel close to you. She'll love having you touch her without having to move on to intercourse. She'll feel cherished, and she'll appreciate that you are touching her because you love her and not just because you want intercourse. Of course, this kind of touching also prepares you both for your times of intercourse.

Showering Her with Compliments

Take a tip from Solomon and compliment your wife often. You can't give too many compliments. Compliment her physical beauty, her emotional beauty, and her spiritual beauty. She is very aware of her appearance and makes an effort to look nice, so tell her how great she looks. Compliment her clothes, hair, and accessories. Occasionally, take her out to ritzy places so she can dress to the nines. Cinderella needs to go to a ball sometimes.

Compliment her verbally, right to her face. Also, share compliments in e-mails, cards, and letters. She'll be thrilled to get these love notes.

Listening to Her

Your Cinderella will find it very romantic when you ask her to talk about her day, her life, her stress, her spiritual life, and how she feels about your relationship. Use the listening skills I taught in chapter 8.

Reading Books Together

Most Cavemen don't like to read. Be the exception. I'll bet your Cinderella would love to read books with you and discuss them. You can read self-help Christian books like this one, old classics, or contemporary novels. Give it a try.

Being Creative on Dates

Take her out on a romantic date once a week. Ask her out early in the week: "Honey, would you like to go out with me this Saturday?" At least for every other date, plan something creative. Something out of the ordinary. Out of the box. Do activities she enjoys: shopping at the mall, visiting an art or craft fair, walking on the beach, having a picnic in the park, in-line skating, going to a museum, playing golf or tennis, bowling...Ask her what activities she would find romantic. Jot down what she says and surprise her.

A Romantic Day

Here's a sample romantic day. It's what Solomon would do if he were still around.

You get up in the morning, lean over to her and kiss her (more than once) tenderly while embracing her. You say into her lovely ear: "I love you, _____. You're beautiful." You make the bed, get her coffee, and help get the kids going. When you leave, you hug her and kiss her several times and tell her "I love you, _____."

You call her or e-mail her during the day to tell her you love her and you're thinking about her. Mention that she looks great in her outfit today. You ask if she has any needs.

You arrive home and do the multiple kisses, the heartfelt hug, and the "I love you, _____." Add in, "I missed you." Right away, ask her what you can do for her tonight. Take care of your chores, do any extra jobs she's given you, help with the kids, and pitch in to clean up dinner. Make sure the kids are in their rooms and ask her to sit down with you for your scheduled 30-minute couple talk time. Listen to her talk, share what's on your pad, and have a brief prayer together.

Enjoy a make-out session or maybe, if it's on the schedule, intercourse. And always remember, kissing, loving words, and foreplay are as much a part of sex and are as important as intercourse. Because of your romantic pursuit during the day, you'll find her a more responsive physical partner. At the end of the day, give her another few real kisses and an embrace and a final "I love you, _____."

Not every day will go this well, romantically speaking. Just do your best. She'll notice you are trying, and your effort will pay off in her loving response.

Marriage Enrichment Steps

1. Caveman, recall your dating days and what you did back then to be romantic. Be honest—have you lost your romantic edge? What are some examples of your antiromantic behavior?

2. Ask your Cinderella how important romance is to her. Ask her how her feelings will change when you crank up the romance.

3. Take some time this week—maybe even right now—to read the Song of Solomon together. Discuss your reactions and insights.

4. What excuses in the Dialogue section have you used to avoid being romantic?

5. Do you have pain in your past or some other reason why you block on being romantic and intimate with your wife? Ask your wife which of my romantic ideas she'd like you to do on a regular basis. Ask her for other ideas she has for romance.

Part Three

How to Fight to Be Close

15

The Screamer and the Escape Artist

Identify and Dismantle Your Old Conflict Pattern

Bill and Barbara are an average American couple. They're decent, upstanding, and friendly people. They pay their bills, go to church, brake for squirrels, and are courteous to strangers.

Barbara is an outgoing, vivacious, and expressive person. She's a real sweetheart and fun to be with. Bill is an easygoing, hardworking guy with a dry sense of humor. He's quiet, steady, and responsible.

When life is good, they get along quite well and are happy together. But when Bill and Barbara are angry with each other, everything changes. These nice, normal individuals turn into the couple from conflict hell. Just like some bizarre science fiction experiment gone bad, a shocking transformation takes place in their personalities.

Barbara, the vivacious sweetheart, becomes Barbara the screamer. She's a Doberman pinscher with makeup. Her eyes bulge, her neck veins swell, and her voice becomes loud and shrill. Little flecks of foam spray from her mouth. She buries Bill in an avalanche of angry, intense words. She's just plain mean.

Steady, easygoing Bill becomes an escape artist. His only goal is to get away from Barbara. He's desperate to escape her clutches. He turns the television on to screen her out, but that doesn't work. No one makes televisions that loud. He goes from room to room, but she follows him like a hunter stalking its prey. Finally, the escape artist grabs his keys, jumps in his car, and drives away. Barbara can just make out what he's saying as he roars out of their driveway: "Free at last, free at last, thank God Almighty, I'm free at last."

When Bill returns, an uneasy silence lingers for several hours. Bill and Barbara never bring up the conflict again or resolve it. By the next day, they are back to their normal selves.

Bill and Barbara deal with every significant conflict this same exact way: Barbara screams, and Bill escapes. Sound familiar? Maybe you are a screamer, or maybe you are an escape artist, just trying to get away.

Every Couple Has a Conflict Pattern

You know something? Bill and Barbara are not the exception. They are the rule. In the first seven to fourteen years of marriage, all couples develop a deeply entrenched conflict pattern. "The screamer and the escape artist" is just one pattern. All couples have one particular way to handle conflict, and it is *not* a good, healthy way.

Your conflict pattern doesn't work! It prevents you from resolving the conflict. You don't ever get close to facing the real issue. You don't even talk about it. The conversation is over well before you address what actually caused the conflict.

The Pattern Itself Becomes the Issue

After the first 30 seconds, Barbara, the screamer, isn't thinking about the actual conflict issue. She's thinking, *You weasel! You wimp! You hurt me, and now I'm going to hurt you. I'm gonna draw blood before you can get away from me. You can run, but you can't hide, Billy Boy.*

Bill, the escape artist, also isn't thinking about what started the fight. He's thinking, *I've got to get away from this Mack truck wearing a dress. If I don't, I'll be crushed to death.*

What's the fight about? Nobody knows. They've forgotten.

The Pattern Is Damaging

You take another chunk out of your relationship. You are a little further apart physically, emotionally, and spiritually. The resentments and bad feelings remain and carry over to the next conflict. You seem to get over an unresolved conflict, but actually you don't. It stays right smack between you and energizes the next conflict.

Let's say you had two unresolved conflicts this past month. If you have a conflict tonight, that conflict will not just be about tonight's issue. It will also be about the last two unresolved conflicts. You'll be fighting over not just one conflict, but all three!

If you want real intimacy in the new relationship you're building, you must do two things in the area of conflict. First, dismantle your old conflict pattern. It must go because it's killing your love. Second, learn to resolve conflict in a direct and healthy way. I'll help you do the dismantling in this chapter, and in the next chapter I'll teach you a new way to resolve conflict.

What is your conflict pattern as a couple? Check out these common patterns and see if any fit.

We Never Fight

Many couples say to me, "We haven't had an argument in our entire marriage." They say this with a straight face, and they expect me to applaud them. They are disappointed.

I respond, "Oh, I'm so sorry to hear that. Did one of you die, and you just haven't noticed?" I tell them that their conflict pattern is called "massive dual denial." "Let's pretend we have no conflict."

The price? No life in the relationship. Many stuffed, buried resentments. Separate lives. In this pattern, one partner usually gets his or her way. That's not a fun way to live for the pilot-fish partner who chooses to tag along with the big fish.

You never argue? No congratulations. You also never have any real closeness or passion.

The Tortoise and the Interrogator

This is the man who refuses to talk and the woman who tries to get him to open up and deal with the issue. When conflict happens, the tortoise pulls into his protective shell and won't come out. He's angry all right, but he won't admit it or express it. The tortoise avoids conflict like the plague. He doesn't leave; he just won't talk. He hunkers down and rides out the storm. He'd rather take a beating than deal with the conflict.

Many husbands play the part of the tortoise. They hate conflict with their wives. They know she's better at conflict. She thinks faster on her feet. Conflict makes them feel out of control, and they despise that feeling. So they maintain some control by saying nothing.

The interrogator is desperate to find out what's going on in the man's head. His tortoise routine drives her crazy. She begins her interrogation, trying to get the tortoise to stick his head out of his shell. She wants him to express his feelings, to share something personal, and to face the issue. She'd settle for him saying anything at all! The interrogator tries all kinds of approaches:

She asks questions. "Are you angry? What are you angry about? Did something happen at work? Was it the tone of my voice? Was it when I dropped the ketchup bottle on your foot? What's your position on the finances? Do you want me to stay home with the kids?" She's guessing, trying to hit on what's happening in his mind. It's 20 questions. Or maybe even 200 questions. Of course, her questions go unanswered.

She's sweet. "Come on, honey, say something. You know I love you. You're special to me. Let's talk. I won't bite. Please? Please?" She even tries some affection to draw him out. Even the chance for kissy-kissy, huggy-huggy doesn't make the tortoise budge.

She gets ugly. "Come out of there, sucker! I'm your wife! Talk to me! How can we solve the problem if you sit there like a lump on a log? Speak! Speak! Have I married a mute?"

Nothing works. That's how the game is played. She tries, he resists, and they both get hurt. The conflict is never resolved. She's desperate to talk about it, but he's just as desperate to not talk about it.

The Attorney and the Emotional Witness

This is the logical man and the emotional woman going toe-to-toe in a conflict. Just like a well-trained attorney, the man patiently and logically presents his case. He goes point by logical point. He expresses no emotion, just the facts as he sees them. "Now, honey, here's the way it happened. You completely misinterpreted my intentions, and then you lost your temper."

He mercilessly breaks her down on the witness stand. He won't listen, he won't compromise, and he won't even seriously entertain her viewpoint. If she can't produce a logical and airtight case, he dismisses her.

He's cool. He's calm. He has the answers. He is always right. He is the source of all truth. He is a huge pain in the rear!

The woman, who is already emotional and upset because of the conflict, becomes more upset because of the attorney's approach. He won't hear her out and reflect back what she's saying. He won't understand and see it her way. He won't consider her feelings. She becomes extremely frustrated, angry, and hurt.

The more emotional she gets, the more logical he gets. She screams, cries, and tries to get him to listen. She fails. Her rising emotional intensity further convinces him that he's right, and she's wrong.

When it's all over, she's angry and hurt and feels rejected. The attorney is alone. He won the case, but he lost the woman. He wonders why she's so cold and pulls back the next several days.

Conflict patterns abound. To identify your couple conflict pattern, think about how the two of you handle anger. You'll follow the same pattern every time you have a significant conflict. Every time.

Catch Yourselves in the Act

The first step to resolving conflict in a healthy way is to catch yourselves in your old conflict pattern and stop it. When you have a conflict, you will automatically move into your conflict pattern. It's entrenched. You've done it thousands of times. It's like breathing. You're gonna do it!

The key is to work together to catch yourselves starting the pattern as soon as possible and stop it in its tracks. If you keep using your old conflict pattern, you'll never resolve a conflict.

The first umpteen times, you'll run right through the old pattern just as always. And as always, you won't resolve the conflict. Later, one or both of you will realize what you've done. Bring it up: "We did it again." Talk briefly about what you did wrong and then restart the conflict discussion with the new approach.

As you get the hang of it, you'll begin catching the old conflict pattern earlier and earlier. You'll be able to actually catch yourselves as you're doing it. This will save time and limit the damage.

Try agreeing on labels in advance: "Bill, you're being the tortoise." "Betty, we're acting as if we don't have a conflict, but we do." "Escape artist, it looks like you're heading for the door." "Sara, you're being the screamer, and I'm shutting down." "Stuart, you're being the attorney, and your logic is making me emotionally intense."

When you catch your spouse in his old conflict mode, say three things right in a row. First, point it out. Second, call for a quick break so you each can simmer down. Third, ask your partner to come back to you when he's ready to start over and try again.

If he doesn't come back, go to him and express your feelings and position about the conflict in the one-way communication style. After you ask him to respond when he's ready, walk away. If he still refuses to restart the conflict discussion, share your feelings about that decision one-way and drop it. Don't bring it up again.

Assuming your spouse will work with you, follow the three steps I outlined above: Catch yourselves in the old pattern, take a five- to ten-minute break, and restart with the new, healthy conflict approach. This is what I do with couples in therapy. I stop them in their old way, take a break, and then guide them through a better way.

Even after you have dismantled your old pattern and have become skilled at the new approach, still you must shut down a conflict right when it erupts. When a conflict surfaces, no couple can immediately launch into successful resolution mode. You're too angry, so you won't follow the rules, and the conflict will blow up in your faces.

The moment conflict strikes, one of you needs to call for an immediate time-out: "Honey, let's take a five-minute break and meet back here." Take a few minutes to calm down, to pray briefly, and to get yourself under control. Then, meet briefly to schedule a time to work through the conflict. It might be in ten minutes, a half hour, two hours, or later that same day. Meet at the agreed-upon time and place and begin the process of moving through your new series of conflict steps.

You ask, "Well, Dave, what is this new, healthy approach to conflict?" We're going to get into that right now.

Marriage Enrichment Steps

1. What is your conflict pattern as a couple? Does one of my examples fit you, or is your pattern different? Discuss the roles you each play in a conflict.

2. Where did you learn your role in the conflict pattern? From Mom or Dad? How did your parents deal with conflict? If you've been married before, talk about how you and your ex handled conflict.

3. What happens after a conflict? If you don't resolve it, what is the impact on your relationship?

4. Agree to begin catching yourselves in your old conflict pattern. Come up with labels for your two roles.

16

Two Persons, Two Truths

My Conflict-Busting Formula

Cinderella and the Caveman have trouble getting along when things are smooth. Living together in harmony and intimacy is tough enough when life is good and no one's upset. Why? You know why by this point in the book. Because of their massive, almost unbelievable differences!

What do you think the chances are that Cinderella and the Caveman will agree on what happened in a conflict and move through the resolution steps smoothly? Zero. Absolutely zero. In fact, it's even less than zero. We're talking negative numbers.

For this reason, Cinderella and the Caveman must learn a new conflict pattern that will help them navigate through their differences to a successful conclusion.

Believe Your Spouse

Your new conflict pattern will be based on one essential skill: You absolutely must listen to and believe your spouse's truth.

When your spouse is talking and expressing her version of what happened and her feelings, your job is to accept what she's saying as the truth. It is *her* truth. It is the way it happened for her. Period.

Two qualities of love in the classic 1 Corinthians 13 passage apply here. According to verse 5, love "does not seek its own." It's not just about you; it's also about your spouse and what she thinks and feels. And verse 7 reminds us that love "believes all things." You need to give your partner the benefit of the doubt and believe what she says.

Is this easy to do? No way! Does this skill come naturally? Hardly. By nature, we do just the opposite. Here's what usually happens.

A married couple is discussing an incident that took place between them one hour before. We'll call them Bill and Bertha. Both spouses were present during this incident. Neither spouse has a history of serious emotional illness. Neither spouse is known to be a pathological liar.

Bertha: "Bill, I want to talk about what happened in the bathroom a little while ago. I'm angry that you accused me of being a gossip."

Bill: (He cuts in.) "Bertha, what are you talking about? First of all, we were in the kitchen, not the bathroom."

Bertha: "I think I know what room we were in. I distinctly remember the sound of the shower."

Bill: "That sound was the kitchen faucet running. And I certainly didn't say you were a gossip. I said I wish you hadn't told your mother what you and I talked about two nights ago."

Bertha: "You called me a gossip and don't deny it."

Bill: "I do deny it. I did not use that word."

Bertha: "Did so."

Bill: "Did not."

Bertha: "You are lying!"

Bill: "Lying? You're the one who's lying!"

This conversation isn't going so well, is? What do you think the odds are that this couple will get down to the real issues and resolve this conflict? Oh, about a million to one. And that's being generous.

They are making the same mistake most Cinderellas and Cavemen make in a conflict conversation: They are fighting over two versions of the same event. Ever do that? Of course you have. We all have, over and over again.

They are quibbling over details and semantics. Who cares if it was in the bathroom or the kitchen? That's a rabbit trail! They are incorrectly assuming that there is just one true version of what happened.

The fact is, every conflict includes two truths, two true versions of what happened. You have your truth—how you experienced the event. Your spouse has her truth—how she experienced the event. You are right and she is right. You are both right!

Please understand you and your spouse will never—and I mean *never*—agree on all the details of an event and what happened. The event could be important or trivial; it could be a conflict situation or not. One Cinderella and one Caveman will always see it differently. It's part of the mystery of being married.

One of you won't say, "Wow, honey, after hearing you talk, I realize I'm wrong. It happened the way you said it happened." No! You experienced it differently. Two different persons always have two different perspectives.

So many couples get hung up on this level. Sandy and I did for years. I tried to convince Sandy that I knew the truth, and she tried to convince me she knew the truth. We stopped our relationship cold.

We didn't get any deeper. We didn't get all our feelings out. In fact, we got even angrier. We didn't get understanding. We didn't resolve the conflict. We got gummed up, and we damaged our marriage. These conversations ended with both of us convinced the other was lying.

We finally figured out how to get through conflicts in a new and better way. A way that protects our marriage and actually creates more intimacy. Our way will work for you too.

Take Turns in Conflict

In my example, Bill needs to let Bertha talk, and he needs to believe that what she is saying is her truth. Here's the replay:

Bertha: "Bill, I need to talk to you about something.

Can you meet me at the kitchen table in ten minutes? Good."

Bertha: (ten minutes later) "Bill, I want to talk about what happened in the bathroom a little while ago. I'm angry that you accused me of being a gossip."

Bill: (He says nothing original. He doesn't say it was in the kitchen. He doesn't deny he called her a gossip and set her straight. No, he's too smart for that. He's learning. He thinks, *I'll try Dr. Clarke's way.*) "You heard me call you a gossip. I can see you're angry."

That's all Bill says! He then allows Bertha to talk the whole situation out and express her feelings. With him listening, reflecting back what she says, and believing her truth, Bertha gets her anger and hurt out. Because he's not disagreeing with her, her anger and emotional intensity go down. For couples to resolve conflict, their anger must subside.

This is the "one speaker and one listener" rule. To resolve a conflict, one spouse must be speaking and one spouse must be listening. If both spouses speak, they won't resolve the conflict and will damage their relationship. When Bertha feels understood and most of her anger and hurt are out, Bill gets his turn to present his truth. Bill does not get his turn to speak until Bertha gives him the go-ahead. He doesn't start when *he* feels ready to talk. He starts when *she* feels ready to listen. That will be when she feels understood and believed. If Bill starts too soon, Bertha won't be ready to listen.

After a short break to let Bertha's feeling of being understood settle and become solid, Bill talks. Bertha listens, reflects back what she hears, and believes his truth. Of course, his truth will be different from hers.

Bill: "I'm sorry for what I did to make you feel angry and hurt. I didn't mean to, but it happened. Please forgive me. What I was

trying to say was I'm angry that you told
your mom about the financial talk we had
two nights ago. I know you didn't mean
anything by it, but I feel like that's our personal business."

Bill validates Bertha's feelings and point of view. He makes sure she feels that he understands and believes her. He apologizes. Only then does he share his side of things. He does not try to refute her view and talk her out of her feelings. He is following 1 Peter 3:7 and being gentle and respectful of her.

Let's put this all together. Catching yourselves in your old conflict pattern is good, but it's not good enough. Listening to and believing your spouse's truth is also good, but it's not good enough either. These steps are not good enough because two more major steps are necessary for working through a conflict.

Stop Temporarily When You've Lost It

When I say "lost it," I mean at least one of you is breaking the rules. You're not listening. You're distracted. You're interrupting. You're too angry, and you're yelling. You are making personal attacks. You're clamming up and shutting down.

You're reverting back to your role in the old conflict pattern, and you are not believing your partner's truth.

When a conflict conversation gets off track, even a little bit, you need to *stop temporarily*. Unless you stop briefly, you are not going to be able to gear down and get back on track. The conflict will get worse, and you'll end up making a bigger mess. It's approaching the point of no return.

Can you imagine the following? One of you says, "I'm angry, I'm out of control, but wait...I'm noticing I have a problem, I'm regaining my poise and control, and I'm lowering my voice. Sorry about that, my dear. Now, where were we?" Dream on. It doesn't work this way. No one can do that. When you lose it, you get mean and nasty. So do I.

The Stop-and-Start Method

Every significant conflict, like every good conversation, is a process. You do not get through it in one unbroken sitting. You need to take breaks when you get off track. Get alone to cool off and process. Let understanding resonate and take hold.

The issues and feelings that arise in a conflict are deep and make you vulnerable. Both the husband and the wife need breaks to think, evaluate, search their souls, talk to God, consider each other's point of view, pull themselves together, and get a grip.

A healthy conflict conversation could last several hours. It's more likely to last a couple of days, especially if it's a big conflict. Ideally, you want to clear your anger out by the end of the first day (Ephesians 4:26), but the rest of the process usually lasts longer.

You must revisit the issue until you've worked it through completely. This will be particularly tough for the spouse who wants to resolve the conflict right away. "Right away" and marital conflict don't go together. Most men are particularly slow processors in a conflict.

Take breaks! Conflict is like a grueling physical sport. It could be an Olympic event, but who'd want to watch? Talk through a conflict in short spurts.

Take a break when you mess up—when you catch yourselves in your old conflict pattern, when you start fighting over whose version is the truth, when one of you starts yelling, when one of you isn't listening and reflecting.

Take a break after one partner has shared his side. Let the fragile understanding you just achieved take root.

Take a break after both of you have shared and understood your two versions of the truth. This break is good preparation for the final step in the conflict-resolution process.

Let's Make a Deal

Many times, talking through your feelings and points of view is enough to resolve a conflict. You don't have to do anything else. But sometimes you both need to agree on a deal, a plan of action to handle the situation.

Making a deal is important, so take a break after you've achieved understanding of your two truths. Set a time to come back together. Process on your own. Think about what's been said. Consider any changes in your position. Pray for guidance. Think of possible solutions and compromises.

When you return to talk, pray for God's help. Make a deal that is specific and measurable. Don't say, "Let's try harder." No one knows what that means.

In our previous example with Bill and Bertha, the compromise might be, "Let's agree to not share any financial information with anyone without our spouse's permission."

Make every deal on a trial basis. If it works, great. If it doesn't, return to the table and renegotiate. Either spouse can call for a renegotiation.

If you don't learn how to resolve conflict, your marriage will slowly die. It will choke on smoldering resentments and bitterness. If you do learn how to resolve conflict, your marriage will be free to grow and prosper. It will be alive and refreshed with closeness and passion.

Marriage Enrichment Steps

1. Discuss a recent conflict in which you had two totally different versions of what happened. How did that conflict turn out?

2. Do you believe me when I say every conflict has two truths? If you doubt this, why?

3. What kind of damage have you done to your marriage by fighting over two versions of the truth?

4. What might keep you from following this conflict strategy?

   - Catch yourselves in your old conflict pattern.
   - Believe your partner's truth.
   - Take turns in conflict.
   - Stop and start.
   - Let's make a deal.

   Which steps will cause you the most trouble, and why?

5. Commit together to practicing this strategy when you have your next conflict. Pray right now that God will help you improve your conflict-resolution skills.

Part Four

How to Kill Your Rituals and Start Over

17

Bury Your
Old Relationship

Change Your Routines and
Drop Your Intimacy Substitutes

I hate to tell you this, but there's just about a 100 percent guarantee that you're going to die before your time. Me too. We have very little chance of living to a ripe old age. Why? Because of all the normal, everyday things that are killing us! Every couple of weeks, another newspaper article or television news report warns us of the fatal effects of some new and hideous health hazard.

High cholesterol kills. Salt kills. Sugar kills. Practically every preservative in food kills. Too much fat in your diet kills. Not enough fat in your diet kills. Red meat kills. Mercury in fish kills. Killer bees from South America are coming to kill us all. They've been coming for 20 years. They're slow bees, but they'll eventually make it.

My own mother played a role in killing me. She fed me margarine throughout my childhood. Turns out it's a killer! It turns into plastic in your arteries. Pollution of the air and water kills. Disease-carrying mosquitoes kill. Secondhand smoke kills. Nonstick coating on cookware kills. Even vegetables aren't safe because they're sprayed with deadly pesticides.

I was dealing pretty well with all these killers until just recently.

Then I saw a television story that said the wrappers for fast food are also killers. That was it. That one sent me over the edge.

The truth is, I really don't worry about all these killers. I take all the dire reports about them with a grain of salt. If they are killing us, they are taking an awfully long time to do it. Yeah, they just might get you in your late seventies or your eighties. Besides, no one can avoid all these things. You have to eat something, or you'll starve to death.

But I do worry about one killer. It's the number one killer of all marriages. Since I make my living working with married couples, I've been fighting this killer for years. It's called *boredom*. I'm on a crusade to stamp out boredom in marriage.

As I explained in chapters 1 and 2, the Cinderella Meets the Caveman marital contract leads to rigid, patterned rituals. The rituals—doing things the same old Cinderella and Caveman way—lead to a terrible boredom. After you've killed your marriage with boredom, you turn to intimacy substitutes. These are persons or activities that take the place of passion with your marriage partner.

We're exploring a strategy that will beat boredom and create an exciting, spontaneous, and fresh love for you and your spouse. You've already read part of the strategy. We've taken a good bite out of boredom by correcting the classic Cinderella and Caveman mistakes. Learning how to fight effectively will also produce passion and closeness. You're well on your way to a new and better marriage.

Now, in part 4, we need to finish the job. In this chapter, I'm going to help you shake up your remaining rituals and peel yourselves off your intimacy substitutes.

Shoot Your Old Marriage

Tired of being bored? Throw out your old marriage and build a new one that works. The two of you can do it together! I tell couples all the time, "Your relationship is awful. It bores me to death just listening to you describe it. Please, put it out of its misery. Take it out back, shoot it, and bury it. Let's start over."

Rebuilding with your marriage partner is God's answer. It won't be easy, but it's what God wants, and He'll help you do it. Part of growing as a Christian is putting off "the old self" and putting on "the new self" (Colossians 3:9-10). The same thing is true in your marriage. You have to put off the old marriage and put on the new one.

You may be on the verge of giving up. Don't! You may think you're stuck with the marriage you have. No, you're not—unless you want to be.

God wants your marriage to work. He wants you to unturn every stone in an effort to build a new marriage. If you demonstrate real faith in God and take the necessary rebuilding steps, He will bless your efforts.

Attack Your Rituals

Study your relationship and discover all the rituals. Read chapters 1 and 2 again to get some good clues. Finding them is not that tough once you start looking. You're like two trees in a petrified forest. Nothing ever changes. The time has come to change your old, boring, intimacy-sapping routines.

Change Your Morning Routine

Get up earlier and share coffee or orange juice together. If you have kids, get up before they do. Beat them to the punch! Or keep them in their rooms while you share a few quiet minutes together.

Shower together occasionally. Two persons can fit in most showers. Why, that's perfect, because there's two of you! I've gone door-to-door in communities all across the United States to research the size of showers. I've found that almost all showers can hold two individuals, but very few married couples ever get in there together. Come on!

Showering together in the morning will start your day with a jolt! It's a jolt you need. You can do a lot of things in a shower besides taking a shower, if you know what I mean.

When you leave home, lay a long wet one on your spouse. A real gum-scorcher of a kiss. A teeth rattler. You're kissing your baby! You're kissing your stud man! And what comes along with that big old whopper of a kiss? Two or three more show-stopping kisses, a sensual embrace, and "I love you, _____."

I actually know married couples who don't kiss in the morning as they prepare to go their separate ways. Standing only ten or fifteen feet apart, they say to each other, "Hugs and kisses." That's about as exciting as being in the bedroom without touching each other and saying, "Foreplay and sex."

Change Your Evening Routine

Go home, carry your television set to the front door, kick the door open, and throw that stupid set into the front yard. Get rid of it! If you won't do that, cancel your cable or satellite service. You don't need 150 channels!

At the very least, don't turn the television on until *after* you have communicated and connected as a couple. Don't give your best hours to that idiot box! You know what that makes you? An idiot!

When you get back together in the evening, act as if you're glad to see each other. Do the multiple kisses, the tender hug, and the "I love you, _____." Cook dinner together. Clean up dinner together. Take a walk around the neighborhood. Play a card game or a board game, just the two of you.

Early in the evening, get rid of the kids and carve out 30 minutes to be together. No distractions, just *mano a mano*. Don't let the kids interrupt you. Ignore their usual pathetic excuses to avoid going to bed. In response to the classic "I need some water," say, "Drink out of the toilet."

Nothing is more stimulating and unpredictably intimate than a conversational and spiritual time together as a couple. Read a couples' devotional, talk about what happened during the day, share what God is doing in your lives, pray, read the Bible, and do some massaging and making out.

Change Your Bedroom and Weekend Routine

Change the side of the bed where you usually sleep. That'll shake things up. Experiment and try new things in your sexual relationship. Be creative and have some fun. Caveman, rig up a branch in the bedroom and start swinging like our old friend the gibbon. If you can't find a branch that'll work, use the ceiling fan. More on sexual creativity a few chapters from now.

Go out on a romantic date once a week and do activities you've never done before or haven't done in a long time. Take turns surprising each other. Rent a sailboat. Fly a kite. Play miniature golf. Take in a community theater play. Volunteer at a local homeless shelter.

Peel Yourself off Your Intimacy Substitute

Just about every married person has an intimacy substitute—a person or activity intended to replace intimacy with your spouse. In the first seven to ten years of a marriage (sometimes sooner), you realize you can't meet each other's needs. You don't know how!

The Cinderella and Caveman rituals have drained most of the passion out of your relationship. Boredom has set in with a vengeance. Since you still have a deep need for passion and intimacy, you both turn from the relationship and develop intimacy substitutes.

These substitutes help you avoid your partner (and the pain and frustration of unmet needs) and meet some superficial needs. But they cause more and more separation and loneliness in the marriage.

Television Addicts

You are mesmerized and utterly fascinated by your television set. You flip it on as soon as you can and leave it on as long as you can. Often, you're not even watching it. It's just background noise. The people on television are your friends and companions. You are living through them. And they're not even real!

Television is your escape, your relaxation, and your entertainment. It's turning your mind into mush! You are a zombie! Is television really that fulfilling? No. Is it better than nothing? Yeah. Yeah, it is.

Computer Hacks

Tippy, tippy, tippy on the keyboard all night long. You send e-mails and read e-mails. You play games. You spend time in chat rooms talking to persons you don't even know. You surf the Internet, checking on your investments and shopping for great deals. Your mission is to seek out new worlds and new civilizations. To boldly go where no person has gone before. To reach level three of the new game you just installed.

You are powerful. You have unlimited knowledge at your command. With the stroke of a key, you can know the mating ritual of the bob-tailed booby. Actually, *you* are the booby! You are wasting hours of time on the computer. You are unavailable to your spouse. You are a techno dud! You are in love with your computer. Admit it!

Pet Lovers

You give your pet more time, talk, and affection than you give your spouse. When you get home, you walk right past your partner, and you're all over your pet. "Hello, baby, did you miss Mommy? Mommy loves her sweetie." You stroke, you massage, and you whisper sweet nothings. You walk your pet, you feed your pet, and you play with your pet. You even kiss (yuck!) your pet, don't you, dog-breath?

If your spouse has a bad cold, you say, "Too bad. I hope you feel better." If your pet gets the sniffles, you're at the vet in record time: "Doctor, help me! Snuggles is sick!"

Loving a pet is a whole lot easier and safer than loving a human, isn't it?

Putterers

You just can't sit still and relax in your own home. You've got ants in your pants. You're always moving, always doing, and always puttering. You feel good when you are being productive and completing jobs. You can't stand to leave any job undone. All the unfinished jobs call to you. Men putter on the lawn, in the garage, and with their cars. Women putter by cleaning, performing a million household jobs, and doing crafts or creating photo albums.

You putter away the whole evening. Your spouse asks you to join him, but you can't. You've got to putter!

These are just a few examples of intimacy substitutes. The list could continue: phoneaholics, kidaholics, workaholics, bookaholics, golf-aholics, fishaholics, huntaholics, churchaholics... Often, an intimacy substitute can be a destructive addiction: pornography, another man or woman, alcohol, drugs, gambling, food, cigarettes...

These substitutes, like all substitutes, are cheap and unsatisfying. Why do you settle for a pathetic imitation when you can have real, honest-to-goodness intimacy? I'll tell you why. You hang on to your substitute because you don't think your partner will ever meet your real needs. You've given up on that dream!

In your old relationship, you're right. It'll never happen. In your new relationship, the one God will help you build, it can happen. It will happen, if you both work at it.

God says (in Genesis 2:24 and Ephesians 5:22-33) that the marriage relationship is to meet your deepest human needs. That's why He created marriage. That's what it's for! If you don't have intimacy, something is wrong.

First, admit you have an intimacy substitute. Don't deny it. Nearly everyone has one. My substitutes are reading, sports on television, and my career.

Second, put your substitute in its place. Its place is beneath your partner on the priority list. Make sure you connect with your spouse *first; later* you can enjoy your substitute. I'm not suggesting you get rid of your substitute unless it is a sin. Just relax with your substitute after you have met each other's needs.

Talk and touch and meet needs as a couple first. That's what the regularly scheduled 30-minute couple times are designed to do. Then you can do whatever you want the rest of the night. Most spouses do their substitutes first and then, at the end of the evening, give each other the leftovers. Meeting each other's needs and connecting intimately is impossible when you're exhausted. You've given your best hours to your substitute!

Caveman and Cinderella, agree that your old relationship is over. Let it go. Say a prayer over it and scatter the ashes. With God's help, start building a new relationship by changing your routines and dropping your intimacy substitutes.

Marriage Enrichment Steps

1. How boring is your marriage? Be honest. On a scale of one to ten (one being super boring and ten being thrilling), where is your marriage? What has made it as boring as it is?

2. Are you willing to shoot your old marriage and start over? Pray right now and tell God you're ready to build a new marriage.

3. Talk specifically about how you can change your morning routine. Your evening routine. Your bedroom routine. Your weekend routine.

4. Tell your spouse (as if he or she won't know already!) what your intimacy substitute is. Are you willing to put your spouse above it? Are you willing to carve out couple time at least four days a week and meet marital needs before you do your substitute?

5. If you have an addiction, agree now that you and your spouse will seek professional help to defeat it.

18

The Best Intimacy

How to Spiritually Bond as a Couple

Meeting needs. Learning how to communicate. Making time for each other. Making your spouse your priority. Connecting with your kids. Being assertive and not allowing mistreatment. Becoming sensitive and gentle. Working to be sexually responsive. Being romantic as a way of life. Resolving conflicts. Changing old, boring routines and letting go of intimacy substitutes.

All these behaviors are important in the process of building your new marriage. But you must develop one more behavior, one more area of intimacy, to have a passionate and truly Christian marriage.

It is spiritual intimacy.

When you are spiritually intimate, the power and presence of God operates at full strength in your marriage. The two of you are no longer loving in human strength alone. God Himself is doing the loving. He will work through each of you to produce the best and deepest love possible on earth.

One-Flesh Intimacy

In Genesis 2:24, God provides His definition of heterosexual marital intimacy: "For this reason a man shall leave his father and his mother, and be joined to his wife; and they shall become one flesh."

"One flesh" describes a complete union of a husband and a wife in three areas:

- physical (two bodies)
- emotional (two minds)
- spiritual (two souls)

This third area, spiritual intimacy, is the driving force behind the one-flesh relationship. Spiritual intimacy taps the power of God and puts it to work in your marriage. If you want to love each other with God's love, you must be connected to Him as a couple. You must join spiritually.

Joining spiritually is the secret to genuine, lasting intimacy in marriage. I call this spiritual bonding. Spiritual bonding is consistently placing God at the very center of your marriage and growing ever closer to Him as a couple.

Here's how to get started on your adventure of spiritual bonding.

You Both Must Be Christians

To spiritually bond, both spouses must be spiritually alive. That means both spouses must be Christians. A Christian is someone who has a personal relationship with the one true God, the God of the Bible, through His Son, Jesus Christ.

As we saw back in chapter 10, the only way to God is through Jesus (John 14:6). God sent Jesus to die for your sins, to sacrifice His life so you could have a relationship with God: "For God so loved the world, that He gave His only begotten Son, that whoever believes in Him shall not perish, but have eternal life" (John 3:16). As 1 Corinthians 15:3-4 states, to become a Christian and know God in a personal way, you have to believe three facts about Jesus Christ: "...that Christ died for our sins according to the Scriptures, and that He was buried, and that He was raised on the third day."

If you have never made the decision to believe that Jesus died and rose from the dead, you can do it right now by saying the words in this brief prayer:

> Dear God, I know I am a sinner. I've made many mistakes in my life. I realize my sin separates me from You, a holy God. I believe Your Son, Jesus, died for my sins, was buried, and rose from the dead. I give my life to You now.

If your spouse isn't ready to become a Christian yet, I still recommend strongly that the two of you begin a spiritual bonding process. Along the way, your spouse can come to know God through Jesus.

The Husband Needs to Lead

God's design (Ephesians 5:22-24) is for the husband to lead his wife in every area of the relationship, including the spiritual. Of course, the wife is fully involved in the spiritual bonding behaviors. You do them together. But, husband, you are responsible to make sure three spiritual bonding actions happen on a regular basis: prayer, spiritual conversations, and Bible reading and study.

Ask a solid, Christian, happily married man to hold you accountable in this area of spiritual leadership. If you can find a man who is leading his wife spiritually, sign him up as your mentor and accountability partner immediately. This could be your pastor, an older man in the church, or a friend around your age.

Your wife will be thrilled with your spiritual leadership. Your marriage will improve dramatically. You'll be modeling for your kids how to build a Christian marriage. Best of all, God will be pleased, and He will bless you.

How to Pray

You can pray as a couple in many different, creative ways. The following practical guidelines can get you started:

Schedule three five-minute prayer times each week. You can pray for the first five minutes of three of your scheduled 30-minute couple times. This not only makes prayer more convenient but also creates a deeper mood and warms you up for your conversations.

Choose one special place in your home to pray. Using the place where you have your couple times makes the most sense. After prayer, just stay where you are and move into conversation. This place must be private and quiet. Get the kids out of your hair. This is not family devotions; it's couple prayer time.

When you pray, hold hands. This connects you and is an outward expression of your one-flesh relationship.

Pray out loud. You're not spiritually bonding if you pray silently. Listening to your partner talk to God is an important part of sharing his or her bond with God. At least one spouse commonly struggles with praying out loud. That spouse can pray silently for one or two weeks. The silent partner can just squeeze his or her partner's hand after praying.

In the beginning, neither one of you will be praying on a deep, personal level. You'll bring up topics that are important but not that deep and intimate. Gradually increase your transparency in prayer.

Husband, you may be too intimidated to pray in front of your wife. She talks better than you, and she probably prays better than you. She may be closer to God than you. The truth is, she won't ever criticize your prayers. After your first out-loud prayer with her, she won't say, "Is that the best you can do, Bob? Why, that's the prayer of a sixth grader! I had no idea how spiritually shallow you are!"

Of course she won't. She will be happy and impressed beyond words that you are praying with her.

Make a list and take turns in prayer. Husband, have a pad with you and jot down the requests you each want to bring before God. When you have a list, divide it up between you and pray one at a time. Here's a sample list one couple used during a prayer time:

- the church's building fund
- guidance for the pastors at church
- the next-door neighbor's illness
- patience with a supervisor at work
- money to pay the taxes
- the children:
  Dan—his grades, especially in math

Cindy—wisdom and protection in her dating relationships

Beth—more friends at youth group and school

- the marriage:

    to spend more quality time together

    to keep praying three times a week

    to have sex at least once a week (his request)

- that Mike would become a Christian

Your prayer list will also serve as a written record of God's faithfulness. As God answers your prayers, jot down the answers and the date God came through.

Spend a few minutes at each prayer session praising God for who He is and what He's done for you and your family. As we read again and again in the Psalms—indeed, throughout the entire Bible—God is worthy of praise and loves to be worshipped in this way.

As you continue to pray together, you'll find that you'll both be more open and personal in what you say to God. You'll pray for your real concerns and the deep desires of your hearts. You'll share intimate things that you will never share in front of any other person.

How to Talk Spiritually

You can spend part of your scheduled couple times talking about spiritual things. Most married couples don't do this, and they miss out on some wonderful spiritual bonding. The spiritual is the most important part of your life, so sharing it will create some pretty intense intimacy. Probably even some passion. Would you like some intimacy and passion? Talk spiritually on a regular basis. Here's a brief list of spiritual topics you can talk about as a couple:

- what God said to you through the pastor's sermon
- how God wants you to apply the sermon
- how God wants you to serve in your church
- how your service in the church is going

- what you're learning in your personal devotions
- how God guided you today
- how God blessed you today
- a verse you read this morning
- how you're doing spiritually right now
- how you're struggling with God and why
- how God wants you to share Christ with your neighbor
- how Satan was all over you today and what happened
- how God is testing you at your job
- how each of you are doing spiritually

I'm talking about discipleship. You are discipling each other! You can help each other grow spiritually. Your marriage ought to be the most important discipling relationship in your life. It can be if you begin to talk spiritually.

How to Read and Study the Bible

The Bible is God's Word. Imagine that! God's actual Word! It is incredibly powerful, and you can apply that power to your marriage by reading and studying it. Also, as a bonus, the Bible can cut through all the barriers between the two of you and bring you closer to each other than you've ever been.

> For the Word of God is living and active and sharper than any two-edged sword, and piercing as far as the division of soul and spirit, of both joints and marrow, and able to judge the thoughts and intentions of the heart (Hebrews 4:12).

If this isn't a great description of intimacy, I don't know what is! If you read and study God's Word together, it will reveal who you really are. When two hearts are revealed, you have intimacy—an intimacy all the better and deeper because God gave it to you through His Word.

You can probably think of many helpful ways to read and study the Bible as a couple. I recommend you start by following this simple and effective plan: read on Monday, discuss on Friday.

Read on Monday

Sit down early in the week—we'll say Monday—and read out loud the passage of Scripture you have selected. Choose a brief passage—no more than three verses. Take a moment or two to silently meditate on the passage. Either out loud or silently, ask God to speak to you through His Word. He'll answer that prayer.

Then take turns briefly discussing your response to the passage. What does it mean? What is God saying to you? What thoughts or emotions does the passage trigger in you?

Cinderella commonly has an immediate reaction, and Caveman may not have much to say. I know that comes as a shock to you, Cinderella. He'll say, "I don't know," or "I'm not sure." That's fine. Don't worry about it. A Caveman takes longer to process information.

Cinderella, don't press him for a response right away: "What's your reaction to the passage, Bob? It's the Word of God, Bob! God and I are waiting, Bob!" Cinderella, back off and give him time to find a reaction. He has until Friday!

At the end of this meeting, do three things.

1. Schedule a time to discuss the passage on Friday.
2. Pray together out loud that God will speak to you through the passage over the next four or five days.
3. Each of you write the passage on a three-by-five card. Over the next four or five days, agree to read the passage at least once a day and meditate on it. You could make this brief meditation part of your daily quiet time with the Lord. You are preparing for Friday! As you meditate and pray for God's insight, jot down on the back of the card what God says to you about the verse. By Friday, you'll each have a few notes written down.

Discuss on Friday

On Friday, meet again to share the results of the meditation and reflection. At this second meeting, you'll both have some things to say. Cinderella will have more to say because she always has more to say. The Caveman will have something to say because he's had time to process.

You each read what you've written on the back of your three-by-five cards. You may share what the passage means for your individual life, marriage, family, career, or service in the church. Maybe God is comforting and encouraging you through the passage. Maybe God is confronting you through the passage. Maybe God wants you to apply the passage in a certain way in the coming week.

Can you see how this plan has the power to create some stimulating spiritual conversations? God will speak to you through the passages you select, and by sharing this intimate spiritual information with your spouse, you will be drawn closer together.

You don't do this every week. No couple is that spiritually minded. Besides, who has the time for that? I recommend doing it once every two months. Go ahead, try this "read on Monday, discuss on Friday" plan. You'll like it. I know God will like it, and He'll bless you for reading and discussing His precious Word.

In God's plan for marriage, sexual intercourse is to be the beautiful and regularly occurring one-flesh result (the climax, literally) of a married couple's ongoing emotional and spiritual intimacy. Every few days (or whatever time frame you choose as a team), the emotional and spiritual needs you have met prepare you to be one in intercourse.

The principles we've seen so far in this book have helped you become emotionally and spiritually bonded. Now it's time for some practical instruction on your physical bond. If you've read and applied these 18 chapters, you're ready to enjoy God's wonderful gift of sex.

Marriage Enrichment Steps

1. What do you know about the practice of spiritual bonding? Have you read anything about this or heard about it in church or in the Christian media?

2. What kind of spiritual bonding behaviors do you practice as a couple now?

3. Do you both know God through His Son, Jesus, in the way I described? If you aren't a Christian, are you ready to begin a relationship with God now or begin an earnest, honest search? If you have honest problems and questions, will you find a reliable, knowledgeable person to help you?

4. Husband, are you willing to take the lead in this area of spiritual bonding? What will make this hard for you?

5. Which of the three spiritual bonding behaviors (prayer, talking spiritually, reading and studying the Bible) are you willing to start doing this week?

19

Cinderella and the Caveman Before the Bedroom

Understand and Work with Your Sexual Differences

The sex life of the black widow spider and her mate is very simple and straightforward. Acting on instinct, the two spiders have sex. The act is brief and easily accomplished. Immediately following sex, the black widow kills and eats her mate. Very neat. Very clean. Very easy.

Some of you ladies may feel like killing and eating your mate after sex. I know it's tempting, but I'm not recommending that. That's not my point.

My point is that I envy these spiders because sex is so easy for them. It's too bad the guy has to die, but it's easy! At least he died with a smile on his face. The sex life of humans is not nearly as simple and straightforward. In fact, sex can be—and usually is—one of the most awkward and confusing parts of marriage.

Here's the bad news: Many obstacles stand between you and joyful, passionate sex. But here's the good news: With the right information, hard work, and God's help, you can build a tremendous sex life. That's what God desires for every married couple.

What you need, dear readers, is an expert with the wisdom and the courage to present a clear, practical plan to produce some serious passion in your sex life. That expert…couldn't be convinced to write this chapter. But he asked me to do my best.

What God Says About Sex

Let's begin with God. He's always the best place to start on any topic.

God says sex is for procreation. Genesis 1:28 and Deuteronomy 7:13-14 make this clear. You don't have to have kids, but sex is the main way to do it.

God says sex is also for pleasure. The Song of Solomon is all about the pleasures of sex! It is stress reducing. It's a healthy release, physically and emotionally. It's just plain fun!

God says sex is also for communication. Genesis 2:24 talks about the one-flesh relationship—a complete coming together of husband and wife physically, emotionally, and spiritually. When we experience intercourse, we can communicate in all three ways.

God says spouses are not to avoid sex but to make it a regular part of their marriage. In 1 Corinthians 7:3-5, Paul emphasizes every married couple's need for sex. If your marriage has problems that affect sex, you need to fix the problems so sex can continue. That message doesn't come from me. It comes from the Bible.

Understand Your Sexual Differences

Before you ever get to the bedroom, the two of you must prepare for your sexual encounters. The initial steps of preparation are understanding your sexual differences and finding solutions to them. In addition to all of our other differences, men and women have major sexual differences.

In addition to the general differences between men and women, couples have specific differences. We'll examine the general differences first.

The Speed of Arousal

For the man, arousal happens quickly. Orgasm can literally be in seconds. The man thinks, *I've got my erection, let's go! I can have my orgasm right now, so what are we waiting for?* There is no buildup to arousal. It's just there. *Boom!*

For the woman, arousal happens more slowly. It takes time. Orgasm cannot happen right away. A slow, steady buildup leads to arousal and orgasm. The woman thinks, *What's the rush? Are we catching a plane in ten minutes?* The woman is not impressed with the man's quick orgasm. She won't hold a stopwatch and say, "Wow! Five minutes flat! Way to go, honey! I don't know how you do it!"

On average, a woman takes 30 minutes from the beginning of foreplay to complete arousal. Thirty minutes!

The Solution

Men, your erection is certainly a tremendous event and very impressive. It's probably the highlight of your day. But it doesn't mean your orgasm should happen right away.

Give your woman more time to become aroused. This may be difficult for you, but it will pay off. She will be more responsive, and making love to a woman who is excited about what's going on is a whole lot more fun. She'll be able to achieve orgasm, which pleases her and you.

Do you ever wonder why your wife isn't into sex and doesn't seem to enjoy it? Chances are you're too fast, and she's not aroused yet! If intercourse happens before she's lubricated, it hurts! Not only can she not reach orgasm—which leaves her frustrated—she's in pain.

Men, your orgasm will be more intense if you wait. The longer you can wait, the better it is.

Keep in mind, men, this 30 minutes she needs to get ready should never be tedious. It's not drudgery for you. You're not waiting, sitting on the edge of the bed: "Are you ready yet? It's been twenty-eight minutes." No! You're touching her. You're loving her. It's fun—the best kind of fun—getting her ready! Foreplay is fun!

Arousal and Emotional State

For the man, arousal is not directly connected to his emotional state. Circumstances mean nothing to the man! After a long, stressful day the man is likely to still want sex. Sex, for him, can be a way to release his stress.

Ten minutes after an argument with his wife, he'll say, "Hey, honey, how about you and me?" The woman is horrified! She can't believe he's serious. The argument and strained feelings are still fresh—not even resolved—and he wants sex? *What's the matter with him?* she thinks. He's a man, that's what is the matter with him.

A hurricane is sweeping across the house. Nuclear missiles are inbound. An earthquake is shaking the foundation of the home. None of these makes any difference to the man if he wants sex. "Honey, the missiles won't hit for another ten minutes. We can do it! What a way to go out, huh?"

His dear wife is in bed, sick as a dog. She's got a thermometer in her mouth, Mentholyptus rub smeared on her chest, and a pile of used tissues all around her. He sits down by her on the bed. She expects to hear an expression of sympathy and support. Instead, she hears, "The kids are watching a video. Let's have sex. We won't kiss because I don't want to catch what you have. I think sex will take your mind off your pain."

She is sound asleep in the middle of the night. But she's not safe from his sexual urges. She is awakened by his groping hands and these words: "Honey, are you asleep?" She'd like to reply, "No, I was lying awake at two a.m., hoping you'd want sex. You've made my dream come true!"

For the woman, arousal is directly connected to her emotional state. Circumstances mean everything to the woman! How she feels personally and how she feels in the relationship will determine how she feels about sex.

If she's not happy and satisfied with herself or the relationship, she's a brick wall—sexually speaking. She cannot respond sexually! How her day has gone and how her man has treated her will determine her level of interest in sex.

If she's had a bad day and something happened that is bothering her, she has to talk it out with her husband before sex is an option. If an issue is unresolved between her and her husband, they must work it out before she can even consider sex.

If she doesn't feel that her man loves and cares for her and listens to her, sex will be repulsive to her. Or sex may feel like just another chore: Make dinner, feed the dog, change the kitty litter, have sex with Bob. Without a feeling of closeness and security with the man, her response to sex—if she even agrees to it—will be, "Well, all right, if you have to have it! Go ahead, get it over with!"

The Solution

Before intercourse, make sure that you have a time of communication and connection. It doesn't have to be that long, but you must have that talk. As you talk in a private place in your home, you each clean out the day's stresses and reconnect as a couple.

When you reconnect, you're ready for sex.

Both the man and the woman need this reconnection. Every couple gets disconnected over the course of a day, and we have to come back together. First comes the emotional rebonding. Then the physical union can follow.

You can't just grab your wife and have sex. I wish you could—I wish I could—but that's not possible. This kind of immediate, "no need for any emotional connection" sex only happens on the honeymoon. And then never again! Let's have a moment of silence for our honeymoon sex…because it's over.

And it's a good thing it's over. With the right preparation, your sex will be five hundred times better than your honeymoon sex.

How Arousal Happens

The primary way the man is aroused is by what he sees. It's visual. For the man, looking at his wife's body gets him excited. When she takes her clothes off, his arousal is immediately triggered. His motto is, "All I need is my wife and a mattress."

The woman is aroused by words, touches, atmosphere, lighting, the mood, and the context. Husband, you may be thinking, *What do you mean by the context?* The context is all the things that make up the experience.

The woman notices the details and is affected by them. She notices every part of the lovemaking environment. She misses nothing. Husband, let me tell you something you're not going to like: Just seeing your naked body isn't enough for the woman. I know that's a shock. In fact, your naked body might be the problem.

The Solution

I recommend you work together to make your bedroom a soft, warm, romantic place prior to intercourse. In other words, make it a love nest! Make the bed. Close the closet doors. Clean the top of your bureau. You want to focus on the bed, don't you?

Put on some soft music. Light a few candles. At least make sure the room has low, soft light. You don't want it pitch dark or too bright. Everybody looks better in low light.

Caveman, get rid of your pile of dirty clothes. You know you have one somewhere in your bedroom. She'll see the pile, and it'll bother her. She'll feel as if she's making love to a pile of dirty clothes.

Also, don't come to bed in your raggedy underwear and 20-year-old stained T-shirt. This ruins the context! She won't be impressed. Play it safe and smart and ask her what to wear to bed. Red big-boy briefs. Superman Speedo. Whatever she wants. No one will know, and it's coming off anyway.

Cinderella, wear sexy lingerie and nighties. I think I speak for your husband when I suggest you get rid of the winter flannel nightgown. It's like going to bed with a pup tent. I've known men who have suffocated in the folds of a flannel nightgown. Or they died of a broken heart because they couldn't find a body in that big old tent.

He wants to see your body. Is that a crime?

As with the Cinderella and Caveman attributes, in 10 to 15 percent of couples, these sexual differences are reversed. The solutions, however, are the same. Just reverse the sexes when necessary.

Specific Differences Between Couples

Some differences are unique to each married couple. Discussing these differences and reaching understandings and compromises before the bedroom is critically important. Consider these four main areas.

Who. Who initiates sex in the relationship? Talk about it and decide which partner will ask for sex. It can be one person all the time or both can ask for sex.

How. How is the initiating done? How do you like to be asked? Let's say the husband's typical approach is to clap his hands together, whisper in his wife's ear "Hey, sweetie, you and me," and then utter two grunts. If the wife isn't wild about this approach, she must tell him what would work better for her. Maybe the husband wants his wife to use these words: "Hey, baby, I want to make love to you tonight. What do you want me to wear?"

When. How often will you have intercourse? All couples differ here. There's no set number. No, wait…a number is forming, coming into my mind. Four! Four times a week! No, not really.

The nymphomaniac craves sex every day. The refrigerator only wants sex once every six months. Although couples usually don't have to face this wide of a difference, it's important to talk about it and cut a deal. If the man wants sex four times a week and the woman prefers just once a week, how about trying twice a week? Work at it, and you'll find a number that fits your relationship.

What. What is pleasurable for each partner during foreplay and intercourse? What kind of touching do you like? Which positions do you want to try? Be specific. "I like _____." "I don't like _____." Keeping your desires a secret ensures that your spouse won't meet your sexual needs.

Talk about what is blocking you from really enjoying sex. Husbands and wives both get blocked. All couples have sexual problems at times. Talk about these areas before you get to the bedroom. The conversation may be awkward and difficult, but it will pay off.

Sex and Kids

Having kids can ruin your sex life. It's a cruel paradox. You must have sex to have children. But once you have the children, you have no more sex! It's over. Their loaded diapers, cries in the night, bad dreams, sleepovers, tendency to stay up late as teens, sicknesses, and a million other child-centered scenarios rob you of your God-given right to enjoy sex.

It's time to fight back and reclaim your sexual privileges. I was thinking of organizing a million-couple march on the Capitol in Washington. My slogan was, We want our sex back. But instead, I decided to provide some practical strategies to keep your precious off-spring from destroying your sexual intimacy.

Schedule Sex

If you have kids, sexual spontaneity is not an option. You've always got to work around your little—or big—darlings. Look at each week and pick the best times. Have a game plan. Carve out the time. You don't write SEX on the calendar, but the two of you decide exactly when you're going to have intercourse. Life with children is hectic and incredibly busy. Sex gets squeezed out if you don't schedule it.

Do It When the Children Are Awake

Don't be afraid to engage in sex when the kids are up and around. Many mothers won't have sex until the kids are asleep. This puts sex off too late!

"I think Timmy is finally asleep."

"Great—what time is it?"

"Midnight."

You don't have to keep your sex a secret. It's okay and healthy for kids to know what you're doing. You don't necessarily broadcast it by announcing, "Kids, we're going into our bedroom now to have sex, and you can't stop us." But it's fine to say, "Kids, we'll be in our bedroom for the next hour. Do not disturb us."

Childproof Your Sex

If you've got the guts—and I hope you do—to enjoy sex while the children are awake, here is your battle plan.

The children are confined to their rooms or another part of the house during your time together. You don't want them huddling by your door. You've heard of those invisible fences for dogs, haven't you? The same principle applies. You tell your brood to stay on the other side of a line at least 20 feet from your bedroom door.

Don't worry about teenagers. If they think you're having sex, they may leave the country. At the least, they will retreat to the farthest corner of the home and cover their ears. In fact, if you ever want to get rid of a teenager who's bugging you, simply say, "We're going to have sex now in our bedroom." The teen will run screaming down the hallway.

Tell your kids not to interrupt you except in a bona fide emergency. And it had better be good. If it's a fire, okay. If a masked man is in the home and they can't overpower him, okay. Make them believe there will be serious, painful consequences if they bother you for no good reason. They can take phone messages: "I'll have my parents call you back. They're having sex now."

Install a heavy door on your bedroom with a good lock. The door seals in sounds and the lock provides absolute security. I've actually had grown men and women say to me with a straight face, "But we don't have a lock on our bedroom door." I reply, "Really? What can you do about that? Wait, I know. You could put one on!"

Forget those flimsy little locks. The twisties and the push buttons can be defeated by a two-year-old. You want a dead bolt. I'm serious. When you swing that big King Arthur door shut and slam that dead bolt home, your kids are shut out, and you are secure in your love nest. It's a beautiful thing.

Another reason for a heavy door with a good lock is to make certain your kids don't come in and see you having sex. That would interrupt you, and it may traumatize them for life. They'll say, "What are you doing? Daddy, stop hurting Mommy!"

Finally, I recommend playing some romantic music during sex. Use a boom box with your own tapes or CDs. Avoid the radio because the commercials ruin the mood. Ads for cars, laxatives, and the heartbreak of psoriasis will drain the passion right out of the room. In sex, timing is everything. Your beautiful background music is pleasant for you, it covers any sounds you make, and it prevents you from hearing the kids.

You're almost ready for intercourse. You understand your sexual differences and have discussed the possible solutions. You know how to protect your sex life from your children. Now it's time to get deeper and more personal as you move toward the bedroom.

Marriage Enrichment Steps

1. Talk to each other about the quality of your sex life. How does each of you feel about it? What's good about it? What's not so good? What are the key changes you each would like to see happen?

2. Cinderella, do you need more time to become aroused? Tell your Caveman how much time you think you need. When you're in foreplay, tell him when you are aroused enough to have him enter you.

3. Commit right now, both of you, to have a time of communication and reconnection before every sexual interaction.

4. What can you do to make your bedroom into a love nest prior to intercourse? Tell your spouse what clothing you prefer.

5. Talk about your specific differences: who, how, when, and what.

6. How are your kids disrupting your sex life? What steps are you willing to take to prevent your kids from negatively impacting the frequency and quality of your sex?

20

Cinderella and the Caveman in the Bedroom

Stop Having Sex and Start Making Love

Sex, by itself, has no energy except raw physical attraction and soon runs out of gas. It can keep a relationship going, but not for long. Just look at the embarrassingly brief relationships of Hollywood stars. Two beautiful bodies, great sex, and then...*poof!* It's all over, and the two stars move on to other partners.

Sex maintains its long-term energy and passion by drawing on your emotional and spiritual intimacy. I hope I've made this point clear. But one other important source of sexual energy and passion is seldom mentioned.

Sex Is Play

That's right. Sex, at its most basic level, is play. Good old-fashioned, free, creative, and spontaneous play. I talk to too many married couples who aren't having much sexual fun. Sex is not a deadly serious drama. It is a romantic comedy!

You and your spouse need to cultivate a playful attitude both outside and inside the bedroom.

Play Outside the Bedroom

Check out Solomon and his cutie of a wife, the Shulammite woman.

They act like a couple of kids all the way through the Song of Solomon. This playfulness is part of the secret to their intoxicating sex. Can you believe this guy is the king? You'd think the king would have to be pretty serious and keep a stiff upper lip. Not Solomon!

Solomon and the Shulammite tossed suggestive comments back and forth all the time. They flirted shamelessly. They called each other all kinds of pet names. They described each other's bodies in vivid, sexy detail. They ran all over the countryside having fun and goofing off. They talked frequently about making love. They made love in more than one place. They talked openly about various sexual positions. Nasty? No! Fun? Yes!

I'm telling you, the Song of Solomon was the original romantic comedy. God, far from being upset by all this sexual frivolity, was delighted by their playfulness. God blessed their intercourse (5:1).

God wants you to follow their example! That's the only reason the Song of Solomon is in the Bible. Its purpose is to teach couples how to maintain sexual passion throughout the life of a marriage. And a big part of the secret is playfulness. So get to work being playful! Both of you!

Dust off your flirting skills. Unless you had an arranged marriage, you used to flirt with each other. Get back to the suggestive remarks. The knowing glances. The sexual notes and e-mails. The phone calls with sexual banter. The intimate little touches that communicate sexual attraction and energy. If this kind of behavior wasn't nasty for Solomon and the Shulammite, it's not nasty for you.

Flirting and acting in sexually charged ways is what makes you a couple! It makes you lovers. Sweethearts. Just a couple of crazy-in-love kids. Anticipating sex and talking about it is healthy. It's great preparation for the bedroom.

Play Inside the Bedroom

Stop doing sex the same tired way time after time after time. On the honeymoon, most married couples find one way that works. A foreplay routine and a position that gets the job done. And that's fine for a while. But by the two hundredth time, it's starting to get a little old.

The same spot in the bed. The same motions and touches leading up to intercourse. The same tried-and-true position. Please! Enough! This kind of automated, repeatable sex is okay for the gibbons and the gorillas, but not for you. You're not brushing your teeth. You're making love!

So, lovers, loosen up in bed. It's not a business meeting. Laugh. Tickle. Wrestle. Pinch. Do some horseplay. Make funny noises. When was the last time you gave or got a hickey? It's been too long.

Try new techniques. Buy a book on sex and read it together. Experiment. "Tonight, the Northern Italian position." Nothing kinky. Nothing off the wall. Nothing you both don't feel comfortable doing. Just something different.

If you can farm the kids out, you can have sex in other parts of the house. That's the main reason for sleepovers, isn't it? To get rid of the kids so you can be alone and free to spice up your sex life.

In the Bedroom

Well, we finally made it. Here are some helpful hints for your periods of sexual activity.

Be Clean and Attractive

Take a shower before making love. Come to think of it, take a shower together. You might never get to the bed! Caveman, this could start the 30 minutes of foreplay. By the time you get to the bed, you'll only have 20 minutes to go before the big event!

Use deodorant, perfume, or cologne. I hate to be the one to tell you this, but your body doesn't smell good on its own. Ever buried your face in a sweaty armpit? Oh, that's fun!

Brush your teeth and use a little mouthwash. If you've just eaten a bag of sour cream and onion potato chips, who wants to kiss you? Even the dog would turn away!

Caveman, you've got to shave. If you don't, it's like being scraped by sandpaper. Maybe your wife likes it rough: "Scrape me, baby, scrape me!" But really, I doubt she'll enjoy your stubble. Her skin is soft and delicate, and your bristles will irritate it.

There is one exception to this shaving instruction. If you have a mustache or a beard and your wife likes it, that's fine. Just keep it groomed. Keep food out of it. If she doesn't like your facial hair, you've got trouble. You'll have to shave it off or wear some kind of a plastic mask.

Please Yourself and Your Partner

When you're in bed together, communicate to your partner what makes you feel good. Your partner cannot meet your sexual needs unless you make them clear. Tell your spouse what you like! This isn't selfish, it's practical.

To make sure both of you get what you need, try focusing on one person at a time for foreplay and orgasm. Flip a coin to see who goes first. "It's my turn, and then it's your turn next." When it's your partner's turn, you are a sexual slave and will do whatever pleases him or her.

Use nonverbal communication to tell your partner something feels bad or painful. It's easy to get pretzeled up in bed. Shouting "Stop that, it hurts!" typically kills the mood. So try agreed-upon signals like a touch on the shoulder or gently moving a hand to a different body part.

Spend Time in Foreplay

Without foreplay, the sex act itself is boring. Extended foreplay is loads of fun and an essential part of the anticipation and preparation for orgasm. Caressing, touching, kissing, massaging, fondling, and talking are all important. Well, not too much talking. Caveman, if you've talked to her before the bedroom, she won't have to talk as much during foreplay. You don't want a chatterbox in bed, do you?

The Caveman can easily focus only on orgasm. His own orgasm, that is. "I mean, isn't my ejaculation the point of this exercise? Foreplay only lasts until I'm ready to do my thing, right?" Wrong! Foreplay should last 25 to 30 minutes, or until both partners are sufficiently aroused and ready for orgasm.

Healthy foreplay is extremely enjoyable. It helps you practice pleasing your partner. It is a wonderful way of expressing your love. And it leads to more intense orgasm for the husband and the wife.

The Caveman might be afraid of losing his erection if he waits. If you extend foreplay, you *will* lose your erection. But you'll get it back. The erection comes and goes during foreplay. Don't panic, Caveman. Don't look down and yell, "It's gone! It'll never come back!" It will come back when you need it.

Have you ever been to a symphony? I've been to a grand total of one, back in college when I had to go for a music class assignment. I learned that an orchestra slowly builds to the climax. The musicians don't walk in, immediately jump to the climax, and leave. They take 25 to 30 minutes to slowly, beautifully build to the big, dramatic climax. That's what your foreplay should be like.

Forget About Simultaneous Orgasm

Simultaneous orgasm is largely a myth. It is possible and it does happen, but only very seldom. It happens all the time on television shows and in the movies, but that's make believe. And you shouldn't be watching that stuff anyway!

Most women achieve orgasm as the man manually and gently stimulates the clitoris. This can happen before or after intercourse and the man's orgasm.

Cinderella, just for fun, try this approach. Have your Caveman husband bring you to orgasm first. Then say, "Thanks, honey, that was great! Well, gotta go!" Hop out of bed and leave the room. This will be payback for all the times he's had his orgasm and left you unsatisfied. Actually, I don't recommend this. Revenge is petty and wrong. The goal is for both you and him to achieve orgasm.

Enjoy the Postplay

The period after making love is just as important as foreplay and intercourse. Stay in bed, relax, talk about the experience, and do some more caressing. It's the afterglow! Don't say, "The ball game's on, see you later." Or "I have a call to make." Many couples scramble out of bed so fast after making love, you'd think the bed was on fire. No! Linger and enjoy!

Caveman, here are some ideas you can use for the afterglow. Pick up the guitar you've put by the bed and sing her a song you wrote just for her. Or read her a poem you penned for this occasion: "Violets are red, pansies are blue, I just love having sex with you."

Okay, I'm kidding. You don't have to go this far. But hang around afterward and cuddle with your dear wife. Hold her. Talk to her. Thank her for a wonderful time. She'll feel loved, not used. And your afterglow behavior will motivate her to desire making love with you the next time.

If Sexual Problems Persist

If you are struggling sexually and no amount of effort and prayer seems to be helping, take two steps. First, get a good Christian book on sex. Read it together and do the exercises. Buy one of the books written by Clifford and Joyce Penner. In my opinion, they're the best in this area.

If the book isn't helping you get past the problem, get professional guidance. Go together. See your family doctor, a gynecologist, or a urologist to rule out a physical problem. If the physical side of things checks out, see a Christian psychologist who has expertise in the sexual area of marriage.

In a high percentage of cases, sexual problems are symptoms of individual or relationship issues. A number of individual culprits are possible: sexual abuse as a child, unresolved issues with an ex-spouse, stress, depression, or poor self-esteem. Relationally, conflict and tension between husband and wife can easily damage and kill the sexual relationship.

Research shows that you can have a vibrant, healthy, regular sex life well into your seventies, eighties, and nineties. Now, if you're in your nineties, you might take all day to get excited. Start after breakfast, break for lunch, enjoy orgasm by mid-afternoon. But who cares? You're retired! You've got all the time in the world!

As you age, making love will take longer. That's okay. You'll just have more time to love each other.

Sex ought to be fun. Sex ought to be intensely pleasurable. Sex ought to be a time of regular, intimate communication. This is God's design. If you follow the principles in this book, this is the kind of sex life you can enjoy.

Marriage Enrichment Steps

1. How playful are you outside and inside the bedroom? Do you flirt with each other? What can you do to get some playfulness back into your sex life?

2. Are you willing to try some new positions in intercourse? What would you like to try? (By the way, there is no Northern Italian position. I made that one up. But there are plenty of other legitimate ones you can try.)

3. Do you both shower, brush your teeth, and smell nice prior to making love? Caveman, do you shave?

4. Talk about your foreplay. Have you gotten into the same old rut, doing it the same old way? What would you like to do for a change?

5. Do you both usually have an orgasm during your sexual time together? If not, talk about how to solve that problem.

6. Bring up all your concerns about your sexual relationship and begin a series of conversations to improve in all these areas. Pray together that God will help you.

21

What If My Spouse Won't Work on the Marriage?

It's Matthew 18 Time

The fun part of the book is over. This chapter wasn't easy to write, and it won't be an easy chapter to read. But I am convinced it contains vital, biblical information for those of you who have a sinning spouse.

I'm writing as if the husband is the sinner. The only reason I've chosen this scenario is to avoid the switching back and forth from husband to wife. I hate using "him or her" all the time. The wife could just as easily be the sinner.

You probably won't need this chapter. Your husband loves you and is willing to work to improve your marriage. He's not perfect, but he is a good husband and will make changes to meet your needs and be a better husband.

But you may be one of the few who has a husband who doesn't love you. At least he doesn't come close to loving you the way you need him to. He is not a good husband and has no intention of making any changes. He is satisfied with your marriage just the way it is. He is a sinner. A serious sinner. Why? Because he is willfully refusing to obey the Bible's commands to husbands.

Two Types of Sinning Spouses

Sinning husbands come in two varieties. First is the husband who is in obvious, flagrant sin: an affair, pornography, alcoholism, drug addiction, verbal abuse, gambling, extreme financial mismanagement, refusal to work outside the home, physical violence, excessive control, manipulation, chronic lying…If your husband is involved in this kind of sin, this chapter isn't for you. Get my book *I Don't Love You Anymore* and see your pastor and a Christian therapist immediately.

This chapter is for you if you live with the second type of sinning husband. This husband isn't into obvious sin, but his sin is just as serious. He has huge blocks to intimacy and refuses to work on these blocks. He will do nothing to improve your marriage. If he says it's fine (and he does), then it's fine. He won't read this book or any other book on marriage. He won't go to any marriage seminars. If he does read a marriage book or attend a marriage seminar, it's a complete waste of time. He is unmoved.

He rebuffs all your efforts to build intimacy. You've talked to him a thousand times. You've shared your needs. You've worked hard to make all the changes you can make as a person and a wife. You've clearly explained what kind of husband you want and need him to be. You've been honest with him about how he's hurt you over the years. You've forgiven him for his past mistakes and continued to keep your system clean of resentments with one-way communication.

If the two of you have met with your pastor or a Christian therapist, the appointments did no good. You've begged. You've pleaded. You've threatened. You've yelled. You've been silent. You've prayed your heart out. And he hasn't changed.

He has dug in his heels and refuses to open up to you and meet your needs. You are stronger and healthier as a person, but he's the same old lousy husband. You are no closer to a personal, intimate marriage.

Ignore the Experts

What do you do now? If you turn to most of the leading Christian "experts" on marriage, they'll tell you there isn't much you can or should do. In fact, these same folks are dead set against you taking any assertive action against your sinning husband. These recognized Christian authorities will tell you to just continue pursuing your husband. Be patient. Be a good, dutiful wife. Smile. Keep on meeting his needs regardless of his behavior. Submit. Pray for him.

This extremely popular advice from well-meaning Christian leaders is wrong. Wrong. Wrong. Wrong. Dead wrong. It will not work. It will ruin you emotionally, physically, and spiritually. It will enable your husband to stay a lousy, sinning husband. Most of all, it is not what the Bible says.

Listen to the Bible

The Bible says your husband is a sinner. A serious sinner. When he knows what your needs are and still refuses to meet them, he's a sinner. When you've clearly described the actions he's done to hurt you and he continues to do them, he's a sinner. When he doesn't respond to you speaking the truth in love about his behavior, he's a sinner. When you have worked hard to correct your Cinderella mistakes and he has no response, he's a sinner. When you've done everything you can do to be a biblical wife and he couldn't care less, he's a sinner.

He is sinning in an intentional, willful way. He has not repented. He has not changed even though he knows what God wants him to do as your husband. With his eyes wide open, he is breaking God's laws concerning his role as a husband (Ephesians 5:23-33; 1 Peter 3:7; Colossians 3:19; Song of Solomon; 1 Corinthians 13:4-8). He has moved from a crummy husband to a sinner.

We know from 1 Peter 3:7 that he is now spiritually crippled. He probably doesn't realize this, but it's true. So he's even less likely to repent and change without some form of direct intervention.

Here's what the Bible says to do with someone involved in serious sin:

> If your brother sins, go and show him his fault in private; if he listens to you, you have won your brother. But if he does not listen to you, take one or two more with you, so that "by the mouth of two or three witnesses every fact may be confirmed."

> If he refuses to listen to them, tell it to the church; and if he refuses to listen even to the church, let him be to you as a Gentile and a tax collector (Matthew 18:15-17).

Your husband has now moved into the abusive category. He is trashing the sacred institution of marriage, and he is emotionally abusing you and, indirectly, your children. God wants you to confront your abusive, sinning husband the Matthew 18 way.

Keep in mind, these biblical actions are the last resort. That's where you are: the last resort.

Confront Him Three Times

Build a support team of friends, family members, and your pastor. You can follow Matthew 18 only with the strong support, prayer, and accountability of these faithful team members.

Gather your team in a meeting and tell them the entire truth about your marriage and what you've done to try to change it. Tell them what you're going to do now. Read Matthew 18:15-17 out loud and pray together that God will use these steps to break your husband and cause him to genuinely confess and repent. Ask your team to be praying during each of the coming confrontations.

Go to your husband and schedule a meeting. Make sure the kids are out of the house when the meeting takes place. At the meeting, tell him he has clearly chosen to not be the husband you need and the husband God commands him to be. Inform him that his choice and his continuing mistreatment of you makes him a sinner. Tell him you are going to follow the Bible and confront his sin. Read him Matthew 18:15-17.

Tell him he already knows what you need. If he has the nerve to act as though he doesn't know, hand him this book. Inform him that you're giving him one week to think and pray about his sin. Make it clear that if he acknowledges his sin and proves to you a heartfelt desire to repent—that is, change—you won't take any of the other Matthew 18 steps. But if he chooses not to repent, you will go on to the next step.

If he shows no signs of repentance at the one-week mark, quickly gather one or two of your closest friends, family members, or other supporters and go with them to confront him again. Do not stall. Move with speed. The clear sense of Matthew 18 is to take these steps quickly, one right after the other. You have waited long enough for the man to change. Do not give your husband any warning. This is a surprise attack. Just show up.

One of these "witnesses" should be a man who knows your husband well. Let this man or another member of your intervention group do the talking. He gives the same message to your husband: "You are sinning. You need to repent and take action to genuinely change as a husband. You have one week to show your wife and us that you're serious about changing."

If he remains in his sin after seven days, go immediately to your pastor and the leaders of your church. Take your "witnesses" with you. Explain in detail the pitiful state of your marriage, the steps you've taken to try and change it, and how your husband is sinning against you and God. Tell these leaders you have already moved through the first two confrontations required by Matthew 18. Urge them to form a team and to quickly go to your husband and do an intervention.

Don't be shocked if your church leaders fail to follow through and deal with your husband. Many pastors and leadership board members will not agree with the assertive, tough-love action you're taking. They'll ask you to be patient and submissive. They'll tell you that if you just love him enough, he'll change. They may even blame you for your marriage problems.

Don't hold your breath, waiting for them to confront your husband. In addition to not agreeing with my approach, they probably don't have the guts to confront. Confrontation is tough, and many church leaders avoid doing it. Some church leaders will confront sinners and exercise church discipline, but most won't. If your leaders haven't done the intervention in three weeks, move on to the next step in God's plan.

Shun Him

Your husband has weathered three interventions—or two, if your pastor and his team have choked in the clutch and done nothing—and isn't about to budge from his sin. Your job now is to shake him as he's never been shaken before in his life. You're at the end of the Matthew 18 process and will immediately and without any discussion "let him be to you as a Gentile and a tax collector" (Matthew 18:17). You won't divorce him. I never recommend divorce. You will first shun him. If that doesn't break him, you'll physically separate from him.

As you begin shunning, gather the children and tell them exactly what you're doing and why. Tell them Daddy is sinning by treating you badly. Give them appropriate, specific examples of his mistreatment. Explain what you've done to try and change him. Read the Matthew 18 passage and describe the interventions you've instigated to obey God's Word. Let them know that you'll be shunning Dad in an attempt to force true repentance. Be clear that if Dad doesn't respond to the shunning, you'll be taking steps to separate from him.

Shunning means that for one full month you ignore your husband. You act as if he doesn't exist. You will only talk to him when absolutely necessary, such as is an emergency situation. Move out of the bedroom. Provide no services to him of any kind. No communication. No "good morning." No time together at all. No food preparation for him. No laundry for him. No sex. You don't sit with him in church. You don't sit with him at your children's school and sporting events. He doesn't exist.

If he's stupid enough to ask why you're doing this, ignore him. He knows why you're doing it. You are obeying the Bible and creating a crisis in his life. He needs to see that he has lost you. You've had it. You're over him and his sin. Will he miss you? Will he want you back? You'll see. A stubborn, sinful husband will change only when he realizes he has lost his wife.

During this month of shunning, begin getting ready to separate from him. You'll probably need a job if you don't have one now. Child care may be an issue. See a reputable Christian attorney (without your husband's knowledge) to determine your rights and what monies you are entitled to in a separation.

If, after the month of shunning, he still remains in his sin, make your preparations to physically separate. Obviously, this may take some time. Tell your children what you're doing and why. Break your silence by asking him to leave the home. If he refuses or is obviously stalling, move out with the children. If you can't afford to move out or have no place to go, remain at home and stay in the shunning mode.

If at any point in the Matthew 18 confrontation process he shows signs of breaking and repentance, be wary and stay pulled back. Do not jump back into his arms. Talk and promises are cheap. You require specific actions. If you've separated, stay separated. If he says he's ready to change, hand him a list of what he needs to do:

1. He'll see a Christian psychologist or therapist of *your* choosing.

2. You both will go to the first session so you can give the counselor the true picture. Your husband will go to two months of individual therapy and work on his blocks to intimacy. He'll sign a release so you can get regular updates from the therapist.

3. He'll meet with your pastor (you'll both be at the first meeting), and they'll develop a spiritual growth program he'll follow for two months. It will include regular church attendance, a small group Bible study, a men's support group (like Promise Keepers), and one-on-one disciple-ship. He'll continue the support group and discipleship relationship for at least one full year.

4. He'll find an older, godly man who will serve as his accountability partner. This could be the same guy who is discipling him. They'll meet face-to-face at least once a week. He will have an accountability partner for the rest of his life.

5. He will work to be the best husband he can be for two months. He'll read this whole book with you, answer all the marriage enrichment steps at the end of each chapter, and apply the principles.

If he follows through on these behaviors and shows real progress after two months, only then will you begin to respond favorably to him. You will agree to enter marriage counseling with him and follow the guidance of this Christian professional.

I hope and pray you don't have to carry out this strategy. But you may have to do it. Don't hesitate. Gather your support team and with Jesus at your side, do it.

Time for Action

This last chapter is a lot to take in, isn't it? You've probably never seen anything like my approach. It is not what the bestselling Christian authors recommend. Your own pastor probably won't endorse it. It's unusual. It's unorthodox. It's difficult and painful to carry out. But it works. And, most importantly, it is biblical.

You can continue to be the good little wife and enable your husband to remain a sinning husband. If you want to end up a bitter, heartbroken, emotionally shriveled-up old woman who never seized the opportunity to experience real intimacy with her man, just stay on your present course. If you want to continue being a sacrificial lamb, a woman who had to get all the pleasure and satisfaction she could in her life without any relationship with her husband or without her husband meeting any of her emotional needs, go ahead.

I'm saying you don't have to live that way. I'm convinced God is saying you don't have to live that way. God does not want you to help your husband stay a sinner. That's what you're doing. God wants you to be the kind of wife who stands up and takes biblical action to change her husband.

You can have incredible influence in your husband's life if you choose to use it. With God's help, you have a chance to change him. With God's help, you have a chance to change your marriage.

Marriage Enrichment Steps

1. If your spouse is in obvious and flagrant sin, please see your pastor and a Christian therapist as soon as possible.

2. If your spouse has been physically violent, take your kids and leave immediately. Call your pastor and other support team members (family and friends) now and tell the secret. Call the police and get a restraining order in place as quickly as you can. See a Christian therapist right away.

3. Do you have a mate who fits my second type of sinner? Are you tired of trying, trying, and trying some more to bring about change in the marriage?

4. What advice have you gotten from fellow Christians and "experts"? Has it worked?

5. What do you think of my "confront the sinner" strategy? What will hinder you from carrying it out? Pray that God will give you wisdom to know if you need to follow my strategy or not.

6. Do you have a good, solid support team? If not, start praying and looking for your team.

Other Books by Dr. David Clarke

MEN ARE CLAMS, WOMEN ARE CROWBARS
A Study Guide for couples and groups is also available

A MARRIAGE AFTER GOD'S OWN HEART
Follow-up materials for couples and groups are also available

I DON'T LOVE YOU ANYMORE

PARENTING ISN'T FOR SUPER HEROES

THE TOTAL MARRIAGE MAKEOVER

THE SIX STEPS TO EMOTIONAL FREEDOM

To schedule a seminar or order Dr. Clarke's
books, video tapes, and DVDs, please contact

David Clarke Seminars
www.davidclarkeseminars.com
1-888-516-8844

~ or ~

Marriage & Family Enrichment Center
6505 North Himes Avenue
Tampa FL 33614

More Great Reading from
Harvest House Publishers

WHEN PLEASING OTHERS IS HURTING YOU
Dr. David Hawkins

When servants of Christ begin to forfeit their own God-given calling and identity in an unhealthy desire to please others, they move from servanthood to codependency. This helpful guide can get them back on track.

101 WAYS TO ROMANCE YOUR MARRIAGE
Debra White Smith

Debra White Smith offers insightful suggestions, "wow your spouse" dates, and romantic poems to spice up your relationship. From lipstick-kissed napkins to romantic weekends, these fun ideas will add zest to your love life!

MEN ARE LIKE WAFFLES—WOMEN ARE LIKE SPAGHETTI
Bill and Pam Farrel

This bestseller offers a unique and fun look at how God made us and the many different ways men and women regard life, marriage, and relationships.

AFTER YOU SAY "I DO"
H. Norman Wright

You'll find a wealth of ideas for enriching your future together in this updated classic, which includes insights on resolving conflicts, setting goals, handling finances, and building healthy in-law relationships.

HARVEST HOUSE
PUBLISHERS

To learn more about Harvest House books
or to read sample chapters, log on to our website:

www.harvesthousepublishers.com

HARVEST HOUSE PUBLISHERS
EUGENE, OREGON